Jumping
Over
Clouds

Jumping
Over
Clouds

Sue Andrews

*A tale of sheep farming,
horses and family*

Crumps Barn Studio

To my family, with love

Crumps Barn Studio
Crumps Barn, Syde, Cheltenham GL53 9PN
www.crumpsbarnstudio.co.uk

Cover images: Clouds © Tampatra1 / Dreamstime.com | Mare and Foal © Dan Tucker |
Sheep and landscape © Lorna Gray
Photographic plates © Sue Andrews

Printed in Gloucestershire on FSC certified paper
by Severn, a carbon neutral company

ISBN 978-1-8382298-1-8

A NOTE FROM THE AUTHOR

When I began writing my first book, *If Clouds Were Sheep*, it originally contained a mixture of *all* of the experiences my husband Aubrey and I have shared during our life as farmers – sheep, village life and horses. I sent the synopsis and first three chapters to numerous agents and publishers. Imagine my delight when, within twenty-four hours I had a response from a publishing company specialising in agricultural themes. The editor loved the book, but as they only published books with farming interest, could I remove all the horse related pieces ...?

I was so deflated that it was several months before I dissected it, removing (but not discarding) all the horse content. Only to discover the publishing house had a new editor and they had a completely different set of opinions.

Two years on I was lucky enough to meet Lorna Gray, the enthusiastic editor at Crumps Barn Studio. She immediately empathised with my passion for our farming life, and *If Clouds Were Sheep* – the story of how we followed our dream to become sheep farmers – was published.

However, when a friend read the script, her first comment was, "But where are the horses? We always think of you and horses!"

This book is the result of that conversation.

It tells the true story of how horses have influenced the course of my life. It also shares some of my own experiences with the sheep, the challenge I faced as a young farming mum raising two children in a remote corner of the Cotswolds, and the unexpected friendships I gained along the way as I and my family began *Jumping Over Clouds*.

I should just add that while some names have been changed, every situation happened, some with more successful results than others ...

My first experience of being in the saddle.
I screamed when I had to get down

CHAPTER I

The South Downs

Was it my love of horses that paved my path through life, or have the people I've met led me to follow my dream of working with horses?

One of the highlights of my childhood were days spent on the South Downs with my parents. The fact these trips usually took place on schooldays only added to the pleasure. My father probably watched the weather forecasts very carefully and planned ahead to take days off work, however I never knew until the bright sunny morning dawned.

My father didn't like children, perhaps me excepted. He didn't like many other people, so didn't enjoy walking on the Downs at weekends or in the school holidays. We rarely saw another person on those wonderful days out.

I was introduced to Chalk Hill Blue butterflies, delicate with their silvery blue colouring. Stag Beetles walked across my hands, while I admired their amazing antler-like pincers, and I learnt to recognise the wild flowers we encountered. Education comes in many ways.

Nine years old, dressed in shorts and T shirt, I would

deliver a note to the school secretary just after 8 am. One day I read it first and was impressed by its simplicity. I would not be in today. No reason. No made up excuse. It could hardly say my parents were having a day on the Downs. No one would be at home at three thirty, so it was inconvenient for me to go to school that day.

We would catch the train to Alfriston, or Jevington which was my favourite place. Central to Jevington village was the stud. I remember spending wonderful summer afternoons just leaning, or probably climbing on, a wooden five bar gate, mesmerised by the beautiful thoroughbred mares and foals that stood together, tails swiping the flies off themselves and their friends, in the dappled shade of the parkland trees.

I loved those train journeys. The route from Hastings to Jevington was hardly used by commuters so there was always a good chance of a window seat. As I stared out at the early morning mist still clinging to the lower ground, sun breaking through to promise a lovely day, my imagination ran free.

My wild horse was with me; jet black with flowing mane and tail. He would gallop alongside the train, jumping the obstacles I selected for him, although sometimes taking a slight detour when the train's route was difficult to follow. If cars were parked at the level crossing as we passed, the morning sun reflecting on glass and metal, my magnificent horse would paw the ground and rear, waiting for the road to clear. Occasionally the train would rush on by, leaving him to sort out the problem, then he would reappear galloping along with ease.

No one else ever knew about him. Why should they?

CHAPTER 2

Real Horses

Although I loved and dreamed of horses, I had to wait until I was about eleven for real ponies to become part of my life. My mother met up with an old friend and discovered she ran a small riding school. After visiting the stables on a lovely sunny afternoon, and meeting the pony I would ride, it was arranged I would have my first lesson the following Saturday.

I spent the next week eating, breathing and sleeping images of Gypsy. Sadly, the following Saturday did not bring an idyllic sunny day. It was pouring with rain. My long-suffering mother rang the stables to see if it was possible for me to ride and to my absolute delight was told yes, the young girl who was helping out that day was quite happy to take me out.

Soaking wet, having walked from the bus stop, I was shown how to mount Gypsy in the dry of the barn. The weather was not abating. We must have made a dismal picture walking the lanes surrounding the riding school for the next half hour. But I couldn't stop smiling. I was the happiest child in the world, even with rain falling from my riding hat and hitting me on the nose. Gypsy plodded on, lowering her head when we turned directly into the weather. She was obviously used to living outside in these conditions. Gloria, who led me, chatted incessantly and was also unperturbed by the weather. My uncomplaining, very wet mother walked alongside.

That day was the start of my riding career. I soon progressed from Gypsy to Robin, a slightly bigger pony, probably about 13 hands high. He was lovely and responsive and I was soon joining the string of ponies trotting off into the woods. But I wanted to canter.

"She isn't ready to canter yet," Miss Benson firmly told the older helpers. Then, seeing my pleading expression, conceded, "She can go with the canter ride, but put her on Smokey, he's too lazy to canter, he'll just trot after the others."

Smokey was a sweet dark brown pony about the same size as Robin, but nowhere near as lively. We approached the area where we could trot away from the helpers and turn at a certain point in the woods, where most of the ponies eventually fell into a canter back to the rest. I held Smokey back until he was worried about being left on his own, then urged him on, keeping hold in front, sitting into him rather than trying to rise to his trot, as my book at home had instructed. He followed his usual stance of trotting as fast as he could, until my enthusiasm met his and by the time we reached the others I was having my first canter.

Suddenly everything changed. We were moving to a new house quite a distance away from the stables. I was heartbroken. Not only was I without the ponies, I also had to start a new school. As often happens, the new school was fun, I made friends quickly, and found another riding school close by.

Soon I spent every waking hour of the holidays at the stables, working hard with the reward of bringing in the riding school ponies in the morning and turning them out at night. I often rode to the field with just a headcollar, bareback and hatless, leading two or three others. Health and Safety eat your heart out! If we fell off, we laughed and got on again.

I also paid for a weekly lesson and, again, a rainy day led to a greater understanding of horses than expected. I'd walked to the stables through the soft drizzle into a full rainstorm, and Katy greeted me smiling, but saying she didn't think we could do any rides that morning. Seeing my forlorn face she suggested I took off my wet things and we had a cup of tea until it eased a bit and I could walk home. Wrapping my hands around the cup, feeling warm liquid slide down my throat to my toes, I plucked up courage.

"Katy, if I pay for my riding lesson today, could I have a stable management lesson instead? How to clean tack and muck out, then perhaps I could help you in the holidays?"

I think she was surprised and probably pleased not to lose out financially that morning. So that was where I first learnt how to muck out stabled horses correctly, groom them and clean their tack. And that was the only lesson I had to pay for. Afterwards Katy used my expertise in the yard and at shows. I learnt where a bit should lie in a horse's mouth, to strip down a bridle and fit it back together and even how to put on a double bridle.

My parents moved house almost every two years, so I

9

found myself somewhere new to ride on a regular basis. Having a sound knowledge of stable management, I became quite useful. I also took every opportunity I could to sit on a horse, some of which were safer than others.

There was a large central park in neighbouring Bexhill where they held an annual horse show. One year they also hosted a country fair with a rodeo display. With Janet, a friend from the local riding school of the time, I took the bus from Cooden Beach, aiming to ride in the rodeo. We were about thirteen, I guess. Janet wasn't sure about participating, but happy to come along to watch.

It appeared to be well organised, although children were riding unbroken ponies in a large open green space surrounded by spectators with merely a rope separating them, so it was probably not the safest of sports. There were about ten ponies, all around 12.2h – 13 hands. I imagine they were unbroken as there were no bucking straps to make them buck, simply the desire to rid themselves of their rider, and nothing to hang on to bar the mane. Rounded up in a wooden coral, the next pony to go was chased into a chute, the rider lowered themselves onto it before the gate was opened and they were loosed.

The event was in full swing when we arrived. Having put my name down to go in the second lot and persuaded Janet it looked great fun and added her name, we sat and watched the excitement. Ponies of all colours came out of the chute, some galloped then bucked, some simply bucked at a standstill and others turned on a sixpence, throwing their rider before they had chance to enjoy the ride.

One older boy came out on a roan pony, kicked it hard so it galloped the full length of the arena before exploding into its routine, thus losing his rider, but not until he'd stayed on longer than the rest. I discovered later he was part of the rodeo, although he pretended not to be. His technique was far superior to any other rider.

The loose ponies were all gathered up in the coral again for the second stint.

"Come on then, missie," the chap shouted to me as he ran a small skewbald into the chute.

"No. I want the roan," I said.

"C'mon, you're keeping everyone waiting. You have this one."

"No. I want the roan. Here Janet, you have this one," and I guided my poor friend forward, where the man helped her climb over the rails and drop onto the pony's back. The chute opened, the skewbald came out with a buck, napped back to the others and shot back into the chute, breaking Janet's arm in the process. Not that I was aware of this at the time, just embarrassed for her that the pony hadn't gone round the ring.

Once they'd extricated the pony from the chute and, I think, dispatched Janet to St John's Ambulance and from there to hospital, I was aware the man was sorting the roan for me to ride.

Climbing the gate, I gently slid onto his back, grabbing the mane in front of me.

"You OK?" he was kind enough to ask. I grinned and assured him I was. As we left the chute, I too kicked the pony hard in the ribs and he galloped almost the full distance of the green expanse before lifting off the ground in anger at the fact I was still on board. I probably only sat out a couple of bucks, but the time I'd stayed on his back brought a roar from the crowd. The ground was hard when I hit it with my head, with no hard hat. Not the ideal landing position, but all I was aware of was that I'd had a great ride and split my trousers.

As the competition continued, I sat on the grass with other friends from the riding school, along with Charlie, the chap who ran it. They told me what had happened to Janet. When the prize-giving took place, I was announced second. Everyone congratulated me, saying the winner, who won the £20, was part of the show. This seemed a little unfair, but by this time my head was swimming in a grey cloud. I found it difficult to focus and wasn't really aware of my surroundings or how I'd got there. Luckily Charlie realised I was concussed and piled me into his car with all the others, dropping me home and explaining the situation to my mother.

I have vague memories of visiting a doctor, who assessed whether I could co-ordinate touching fingers of my right hand to my left. I think the verdict was I'd be alright in the morning and was sent home to sleep it off.

My short-lived career as a rodeo rider.
Incredible that someone captured the moment

CHAPTER 3

Working with horses

My desire for an equestrian career was thwarted initially by my parents, who felt secretarial training would prove more secure. However, the minute I qualified I worked with horses full-time. The jobs were varied; some good, some appalling, but from each I gained experience.

My first job at a riding school in Surrey, I found from the local paper. I may well have been the only person who applied for the job, but I got it. At the interview I was introduced to several girls who were already working there, but when I started, they'd all disappeared. For the first four weeks it was only Sheila, a qualified teacher and me, with ten stabled horses, eighteen riding school ponies at grass and lessons to give daily. Eventually we were joined by others, but it was a fairly steep learning curve.

Initially I simply exercised the livery horses, after we'd caught up the riding school ponies in the morning, leaving Sheila to manage the lessons. Once we gained more staff, I took on some of the younger children's lessons, forming quite a rapport with several. This proved especially helpful when I lost a horse one day.

The owner of a grey cob, Merry, had a friend coming to ride him, which was welcome news as we were so busy. Not only did she ride him, but also cleaned his tack and put it away. Perhaps if she hadn't done this, I would have noticed the problem. Early the following morning, a Saturday, I rode out on Mist leading Merry, attempting to get most of the exercising done before the lessons started. It was a lovely morning, crisp, with frost still sparkling on the verges. As I rode along one of the small lanes, bounded by many elegant, expensive houses, something spooked Merry, who pulled back on his bridle, leaving me holding the reins, bit and cheek pieces, while he took off in just his head piece and browband. The grass on one of these manicured lawns was more than he could resist, his heavy feet indenting into the immaculate turf. I rode up the drive after him, wondering how I was going to recapture Merry without Mist's hoofmarks adding to the problem when a gold Rolls Royce swept onto the gravel. My heart sank. The passenger door swung open and a small girl, with shoulder length brown hair, jumped out.

"Daddy, Daddy. Do something. Sue's lost Merry." There was one of my star pupils, Diana, instructing her father to assist me. Could I do anything but smile? I apologised and explained what had happened. The poor man was left holding Mist while Diana ran into the house, returning with sufficient carrots to temp even Merry away from the glistening grass. When we'd caught him I discovered the problem. He'd obviously pulled back on his bridle from something secure and bent the prongs in the cheekpiece buckles. Diana found a dog lead to use as a running repair. I felt for her poor father staring at his damaged lawn, with his daughter assuring him that the gardener would put it right.

Thank goodness, she was obviously the light of his life, and as her friend, I was excused. I later discovered Merry's owner's friend had tied Merry to a gate while she'd had coffee with someone and he'd pulled back and damaged the bridle. Just a pity she hadn't mentioned it.

There was certainly variety in my life, from teaching riding in a boy's prep school, to working in a dealer's yard, where I was first to ride anything that came in, safe or not. I certainly learnt to sit tight! A year on a small Thoroughbred and Welsh pony stud gave me Grand National winner Lucius to handle as a foal and his mother, Matches, to hunt.

Matches was a super National Hunt mare, who produced a number of top-class progenies, although Lucius must always be her best. She wouldn't get in foal while suckling, so became my hunter for the year that she bred him. We also supplied palomino Welsh ponies for Chipperfield's circus. Finally, I landed the job destined to change my life, with world-famous showjumper Pat Smythe.

*Competing on Pat Smythe's stunning
palomino stallion*

CHAPTER 4

Pat Smythe

Pat Smythe was every pony-mad, small girl's heroine during my childhood. I knew all her books from cover to cover; the *Three Jays* series and her autobiographies, perhaps the most famous was *Jump for Joy*. She has to be the greatest woman show jumper ever. She saw accurate strides to a jump and had hands of silk, allowing her horses every chance to extend over big fences. Her most famous horses – Tosca, a grey mare, and Price Hal, a chestnut ex-racehorse gelding – were bought cheaply, but both became world class show jumpers. In 1956, not only was she the first woman to compete at the Olympics show jumping event, but she also went on to win Bronze.

The chance to work for her seemed more of a dream than actuality. And if the job I'd been offered in Austria, working with dressage horses, hadn't been cancelled, my life would have taken a completely different direction.

Suddenly let down, with no job or accommodation, I scoured *Horse and Hound*. That week there were only two jobs worth considering, both far away from home, in the Cotswolds. I applied for and was invited to interviews at both, but chose to visit Pat first. Paddy, her secretary greeted me at Kemble station, and we drove back through picturesque landscape to Pat's beautiful manor house. I felt I already knew Paddy from my avid reading of all Pat's books.

There were three of us being interviewed that day; three had visited the day before. The job involved working with head girl Mary, bringing on Pat's youngsters she'd bred from her great showjumper Tosca and Tosca's first daughter, Lucia, both of whom were still at stud. We all rode several horses in the indoor school and lunged an older horse, then popped another round a course of show jumps. By now I'd realised the others were more experienced than me, but decided I'd just enjoy my day out. My departure train was later than the other girls, who already had a lift to the station. Then to my surprise Pat asked me into her office and offered me the job. Apparently, my laid-back approach won the day.

It really was a job of a lifetime. With tuition from both Pat and her husband Sam, himself a top Swiss three-day event rider, and a string of talented horses, I was in heaven. I spent a wonderful eighteen months at Sudgrove, just outside Miserden, producing young horses and riding Pat's lovely 14 hand palomino stallion. He was a competition star in his own right, as well as siring several riding ponies Pat produced from her small stud of Welsh mares, most of which sold to Switzerland. He was also a wonderful hunter, giving me great days out, especially when the whipper-in needed a lead over jumps.

The job was life-changing in a different way too – because it was here in Gloucestershire I met Aubrey.

Our marriage brought the job to a close. Pat needed someone who could live-in at the yard, and Aubrey and I needed greater finance while Aub finished his apprenticeship. However, our connection to Pat didn't end there, because many years later, as Aub and I followed our dream to become sheep farmers, a lucky chance led us to rent her farm at Sudgrove.

With Aubrey, at a show at Gloucester market,
early in our Texel breeding journey

Chapter 5

Winter

Aubrey and I have been raising our family and our flock of sheep in this corner of the Cotswolds for over forty years now. We began our farming lives at Througham, and now we live on the edge of the nearby village of Miserden, while still farming Pat's farm at Sudgrove.

January on the farm isn't my favourite month. Not the worst: November, if it's dank and grey, can look at you, giving warning that its miserable weather could be with us for the next five months. So, January scores there! It's not so long until spring.

Some winter mornings, the ground is hard and crisp, with hedgerow foliage sparkling in the early sunlight. Hawthorn berries and roseships might peak out from Old Man's Beard and frosted brambles. Sometimes, a haze rises from the valleys as the sun breaks through.

In December 2018, it was so cold as the year drew to a close that the ponies often had frost shining on their thick shaggy coats. Luckily, the sheep were able to stay out until the beginning of January, as the ground was hard and cold enough for the feed to be taken out to them on the JCB. Then we listened to the Countryfile weather forecast and decided enough was enough. Heavy snow was forecast, and they were right. When we walked the main mob of ewes very quietly back across the valley from their field on the far side, the depth of snow we'd already had meant they walked double file in the compressed tracks the tractor tyres had left.

Speed was of the essence in getting them inside, as that night we had a further six inches of snow to add to that already on the ground. Two days later, we sorted those scanned carrying twins from those carrying singles so the feeding regime could be directed at the correct ewes. Those with triplets, and the two with quads, had been put in the old grain store prior to the first fall of snow, as they were the ones more susceptible to stress.

This winter, by contrast, an ark was really the order of the day. Farming really is a life of extremes and I don't think the weather ever repeats the same pattern twice. Some days feeding the sheep seemed such a chore it was hard to drag ourselves out of the house, but we did. We thought it would never stop raining.

Everywhere was mud. When we fed those still outdoors, which was the majority, their troughs were full of water and we were covered in mud emptying them daily. Fortunately, they all had some shelter along hedges and walls, and when we repositioned the fresh large hay bales, they lay on the remains of the last one, somewhere slightly drier.

The only enthusiastic one was Maisie, our young sheepdog. She loved life every minute of the day. Being a short-coated collie, she cleaned up easily whatever the weather conditions – unlike our older and saner dog Jill, who had the coat of a bear. I'm sure it kept her warm while it was dry, it just took some cleaning off now that she was wet and muddy.

Eventually, we decided the tractor was making such a mess taking hay and feed out to the in-lamb ewes that a decision had to be made on whether to bring them into the shed early. Still five weeks away from lambing they don't benefit from restricted exercise for that length of time. In fact, lambing is noticeably easier when the weather is good enough to leave them out until just before they are due. It must stop raining sometime. Mustn't it?

A friend on social media asked when were we going to get a proper winter with cold and snow. I replied probably about the 18th February when we started lambing ...

I'd rather it just stayed wet though. The cold can be so destructive. Iced-up water troughs both in the buildings and all around the farm take so much time out of the day to defrost and moving sheep is hazardous on concrete yards. I'm definitely a summer person.

Dragging on my wellies yet again, I remembered a poem I had seen on Facebook, and rewrote it to suit my situation:

> *Tell me again why I do this*
> *The rain's beating hard on my face*
> *I'm trying to fill the hay feeder*
> *I need to quicken my pace.*

The rams are swimming towards me
Arm bands and snorkels aplenty
I'm getting too old for this crap
Seemed wonderful when I was twenty.

I'm cold and my fingers are numb
The sheep don't care for my whining
I'd like to be home in the dry
With a warm man, and simply fine dining.

Come on Sue, you know you're not beaten,
Only the ewes left to check
You can bet they are just as unhappy
With mud right up to the neck!

(after the poem by goat keeper Natasha Main)

Soon the weather forced us to bring the ewes in. Then the year's lambing began with a disaster. A ewe carrying triplets barged her way into the feeders, getting badly squashed and throwing out a water bag. This was all quite unnecessary as there was plenty of space for the ewes to feed, but no, she wanted to be in a certain position in the feeder, and there wasn't room. Further down there was plenty of food and room to get to it, but try explaining that to a greedy Texel. This meant the onset of a birth, even though she wasn't due for another three weeks. Because she wasn't ready to give birth naturally, we needed a caesarean. We can't just leave well alone because the loss of a water bag indicates at least one of the lambs would die, and this is turn will prove toxic to the other lambs and the ewe.

All three lambs were healthy and born alive, but gradually we lost them all, one lasting 36 hours. Premature lambs don't have their lungs sufficiently formed to survive. I knew I was fighting a losing battle, but in these situations, I always have to try. At least the ewe was well and would lamb again the following year, hopefully at the correct date.

Last autumn we'd taken the rams out after a month, putting them back with both pedigree and commercial ewes later, to lamb in April. Then, in the middle of January these later ewes were scanned, revealing high pregnancy rates. We could anticipate three lots of quads and several triplets, the April flock lambing to over 200%. Hopefully the weather would have improved by then! Luckily it did.

The timing of when we put the rams in with the flock is actually carefully planned – a ewe's gestation period is roughly 145 days, so we can usually be pretty confident about when lambing will begin in the following spring. A few years ago, we planned even more carefully than ever because Aubrey needed to attend the Paris Agricultural Show for a couple of days. It would have been too much for him to work through lambing followed by dashing straight off to Paris at the end of February – and hopefully he'd be back before the main flock lambed – so instead we'd put the rams out two weeks later than usual, delaying lambing until the start of March.

The previous autumn we'd been asked to provide two

rams for the Texel stand at the show, which had been sold to a French purchaser, so Aub flew over to the Paris with Steve, Chief Executive of the Society. Lambing started slowly on Sunday, the day Aubrey left, but by Tuesday we were well underway. I had two students helping, one knowledgeable, the other learnt quickly. Tuesday was just like mid-summer, and single lambs born on the previous two days were turned out during the day, although it was easier to bring them in at nights from a feeding point of view.

My evening calls from France relayed details of the good time Aub was having with Steve

"It's work Darling, exports, trade. You know someone's got to do it."

Oh yes.

"Did you order more ewe nuts before you went?" I asked.

"Oh, no. Can you do it? Jeff's details are on the board in the kitchen."

"Hang on a minute." Putting the phone on the table, I started to flick through all the notes pinned to the cork board. I felt sure all the information was there. Typically, just as I found what I was looking for, wads of papers and envelopes fell to the floor.

"Yeh, it's here. Four tons?"

"Yes. You're a star."

As the phone cut off, I sat on one of the kitchen chairs and surveyed the pile of useless information that had fallen from the board. After retrieving two receipts from the cat's bowl and a Christmas drawing from Toby, our oldest grandson, I sorted an enormous pile of what needed keeping from what should have been binned months ago and dealt with it.

I ordered the feed the following morning, when I finally remembered what I'd set out to do in the first place.

While Aub was away, lambing continued with its usual challenges. Lambs born from an easy birth could sometimes decide life was not worth fighting for, and took a lot of persuading that breathing becomes habit-forming after a while. Others were up and sucking immediately. Sometimes one ewe would have triplets at the same time as another had a single, and a wet adoption could be attempted. One lamb is taken from the triplets, wiped in the afterbirth of the single's lamb, then both are presented to the ewe, and generally she will accept and love both lambs. A successful outcome for both families.

Feeding the ewes became a frenzy similar to offering free hot dogs to a football crowd. It presented even more challenges with ewes in lambing pens, which were set up in part of the sheep shed as temporary accommodation for those who had lambed at night. Later, they would be taken to the other barn. But first it was breakfast-time.

The ewes in pens were always fed first, but while Aub was living it up in Paris, I had to cope with a particularly greedy large white Texel ewe who decided she had to have her neighbour's food, even though her own food was in her pen.

Unfortunately, she was penned in by one of our old wooden hurdles, which disintegrated as her bulk landed on it. Not to be outdone, the smaller Blue Texel ewe, in the pen next door, decided to put her head through the ruined bars of the hurdle and tried to eat the food in the other pen. Sadly, the Blue couldn't reach. Nor could she extricate her head, so I had two pairs of confused lambs in pens with different mothers, or parts of them.

Luckily, I quickly found a hammer and dismantled the wooden hurdle leaving both ewes in the same pen. Their lambs stood at the back out of harm's way, as I undid the front hurdles and loosed both ewes into the alleyway. This was all happening to uproar in the main shed, as I was halfway through the feed ritual. I abandoned these two and continued feeding some better-behaved sheep in the remaining pens, and the main flock in the other bigger pens. Eventually I found a new metal hurdle to separate the ewes and all were contained again.

The following couple of days were cold, with all going quiet in the shed, apart from some very vocal triplets who were hopeful that a bottle would be arriving every time they saw me, even though they had just been fed.

One of the old Blue Texels constantly defied gravity – she tended to sleep leaning against one of the gates, just managing not to fall out on a regular basis as we opened it to pass in and out. Although the ewes had not been in long, the level of straw bedding in the shed was higher than the ground outside, so her balance was to be admired. She was a determined old bird with no thought of sitting elsewhere.

On Sunday afternoon, after Aub's return, we were tagging and tailing some lambs when we heard sheep baaing in the bottom field. On investigation we discovered a lamb had become separated from its mother and had had its throat ripped open. A classic dog attack. Two days old. Such a short life. The needless destruction of a pedigree ewe's annual return, and a tragic personal loss for both us and the poor ewe. Another dog owner with their harmless pet off the lead, probably unaware of what it had done until it returned to them covered in blood.

Wednesday evening and all looked quiet, so we anticipated an early finish, until one of the ewes that had lambed that morning prolapsed her uterus. We called the vet who, fortunately, was able to get to us in about 30 minutes, while we wrapped her uterus in a warm, damp towel to keep as much infection out as possible until he arrived and re-inserted it! Amazingly, with a cocktail of painkillers and antibiotics, she made a full recovery and was soon out in the field rearing her lambs.

And then, suddenly, as often happens in farming, the pace of life eased. The evening sunshine was making our farm look its very best, casting long shadows across the hills. Well grown lambs were skipping around the fields while their mothers grazed, and all seemed well with their world. I was looking at a scene that has been found in our Cotswold hills for centuries.

CHAPTER 6

Caught in the Snow

We've lived in Miserden or close to it in Througham for most of our married life. Set right on top of the Cotswolds, over 700ft above sea level Miserden is a true step back in history, harking back to feudal times. The entire village, apart from the Carpenter's Arms and village school, is still in the ownership of Misarden Park, as it has been for centuries.

It's built in the grey limestone of the area, which could sound drab. However, it's one of the most picturesque villages around, with a huge sycamore tree in its heart, run and cycled round by generations of children, including ours.

The Cotswold hills are higher than most think. Not renowned for their height, like the Welsh mountains or the fells in the North or the Scottish hills, the unwary can be surprised by the freak weather systems. Race-goers at Cheltenham on a sunny afternoon often comment on the surrounding hills vanishing under deep cloud or snow – and when snow comes to us it can appear suddenly, with amazing strength.

I got a taste of that back in the mid-seventies, when we first moved to Througham.

At that time, before we had our first sheep, I was working for Laura, an interior designer who needed help with her family's horses and ponies. My job was to feed, muck out, and exercise them.

She lived near Cirencester, less than ten miles away and probably half that as the crow flies, but being over 300ft lower than Miserden and Througham, the weather there could be totally different.

January had been sharp and crisp and the sudden sight of snow falling caught me unawares. I'd been strenuously grooming Hector, one of the horses, and felt considerably warmer than I had earlier in the day. The effort I was putting into my work masked the rise in temperature often associated with snow. As I threw his rugs over him, making sure they were comfortable and secure for the night, I was surprised to see the large white flakes floating through the air outside his stable.

Gathering up my grooming kit, I headed for the tack room and glanced at the clock. It was only half past two but the sky had darkened sufficiently for me to think it far later. Moving into the feed room I collected the hay nets, giving one to each horse, then made the decision to mix small chaff evening feeds with carrots, nothing that would harm them should they be stable bound the next day. Still wondering if I was making too much of the situation, I became aware of the immense size of the flakes and popped my head into the house.

"Laura, I've put their feeds in and I'm going to make tracks," I called. "It's just beginning to snow quite hard. Might be worse at home."

"OK. No problem," said Laura appearing from the kitchen, tea towel in her hands. She poked her head out of the door and looked up at the sky and frowned. "It is coming in a bit dark, yes, you go. If it's bad tomorrow I'll just give them hay and keep them in."

Gathering Florrie, our trusty Bearded Collie, into the truck, sitting in the passenger seat as he preferred, I drove out of the yard. Florrie always came to work with me, his greatest joy was being able to run alongside when I exercised the horses, a mass of grey and white hair and long tongue lolling out of the side of his mouth. Though similar in appearance to an Old English sheepdog, but with a tail, I liked to think he was more intelligent.

Our ancient Toyota pickup (more rust-coloured than the blue stated on the log book) skidded a bit as I turned to drive up the small hill from Laura's. Florrie sat beside me, totally fascinated by these odd white things falling out of the sky, he tried hard to catch them through the windscreen with a large furry paw, making driving even more hazardous.

"You're an idiot," I said to him. "I'd rather you didn't try to play with the wipers."

The snow was settling on the road. Trying to remember everything Aub had said about driving in bad conditions, I kept the truck in as high a gear as it would take. Easing back as we approached the main road, I was pleased to see no traffic. I could keep the truck moving.

The snow was falling with far more determination now, the wipers going at full pelt to clear the windscreen. I just had the valley to go down, then up the other side which was the slight worry. The single-track road, although snow covered, was still frozen underneath so I crept down the hill in low gear. Florrie was now sitting quietly, possibly feeling the tension of the situation.

At one point the truck slipped when I touched the brake for a second, but as it knocked into the verge, it straightened up and I breathed a sigh of relief rounding the bend at the bottom. With my speed consistent I managed to keep going up the first part of the hill. The road then levelled off slightly, which gave the truck a little more impetus to take on the second half. Suddenly the wheels were sliding. The pick-up was no longer going forward. I managed to guide it into the hedge where the road was widest and we ground to a halt. Damn. What now? I thought.

"Looks like it's your lucky day, Florrie. It's walkies." I fondled his ears, glad of his companionship.

Already dressed in full waterproofs, I pulled my woolly hat well down over my ears, put on my gloves and with Florrie beside me, started to walk for help. All around was silent. The snow was heavier now. The grey pillowed sky appeared to sigh as it gratefully shed its load. Even Florrie appeared to be slightly anxious. I was amazed at the speed with which the landscape had changed with the snow now at least a couple of inches deep.

I was only about a mile from Miserden, where we used to live and I headed on up the hill to a stile which opened onto a footpath to the village pub. Although it was now after three, being Saturday I was hopeful the pub would still be full of lunchtime drinkers. Licensing hours are not strongly adhered to in the country. Someone was sure to have a land rover that could pull me to the top of the hill. Although I still had another four miles to go, it was fairly level from there on and hopefully, I should make it.

The climb seemed interminable, although Florrie thoroughly enjoyed it. Once he realised the snow was more friend than foe, he was totally juvenile, pouncing on snowflakes, biting the snow then throwing himself on his back, waving his long hairy legs in the air.

"Stupid dog," I laughed at him, feeling much happier.

I found the stile. The overhanging trees on the footpath had sheltered it from most of the snow, making the going easier. I could see lights and hear voices before I crossed the village square. The whole place looked like a Christmas card: grey limestone buildings shrouded in a silken white coating, golden lights showing in several cottages and the fairytale wisps of smoke curling from the chimneys and disappearing into the grey sky.

I opened the pub door. Jubilant whoops were heard as Florrie and I appeared. I unwrapped myself and we both shed a fair amount of melting snow on the carpet.

"Come in, come in. You must be frozen," were the greetings. In actual fact I was roasting having ploughed through deep snow up hill, and glad to shed a layer.

"Here, have a cider," and one was thrust in my hand, I wasn't sure who from. I was obviously a new highlight and source of entertainment for the bored Saturday afternoon drinkers.

"Has it started snowing now then?" someone enquired.

After several of the drinkers had peered out of the door, they came back in. "It's snowing hard out there. We'd better make tracks or we won't get home."

"There's worst places to get stuck, Tom. I'm quite partial to this fire," said someone else. I had to agree the roaring log fire was most inviting. Florrie had already settled himself in front of it and was licking the snow balls off his paws, though he didn't stay close for too long.

"Please could someone give my truck a pull up the hill before you all disappear?" I appealed. "It wouldn't make it to the top of Bull Banks so I've walked from there, but I'd like to get home if I can."

"'Ave you really? Where you been? Where you going?" The questions were fired at me, and then Mervyn, who with his wife Kath ran the Carpenter's Arms at that time and knew us well, shouted to someone in the bar.

"This young lady needs a hand, Roger. You've got your land rover, haven't you? Can you give her a pull, then p'raps you could follow her part way home, she's going the same way as you?"

Roger turned out to be a helpful farmer from Stroud, and I was soon loaded in the front of his vehicle, Florrie safely shut in the back. Two Jack Russells sat on my lap, one of whom felt he needed to kiss me most of the way back to Bull Banks. I hadn't realised just how heavily the snow was falling or how dark it had become; it was difficult to make out the truck.

"Crikey, how long you been here?" Roger asked.

"Well I only walked to the pub, so I suppose about forty-five minutes. It's really blowing and coming down now, isn't it?"

With some technical manoeuvring, Roger eventually turned his land rover round in the road, slightly hampered by the fact that I'd left the pickup in the most useful place for turning. He linked a chain between the two vehicles and told me to get in mine, take the handbrake off, knock it out of gear and steer, which I did most gratefully, taking Florrie with me. I shivered, missing my Jack Russell blankets, but was soon a lot happier when I'd been towed to the top of the road where I had a fairly level route home.

"Drive carefully, this wind'll have whipped up some drifts," warned Roger. "I'll be behind you 'til you get to the Througham turning, but don't end up in a ditch, will you?"

Thanking Roger profusely, I took on board his warning. It was nearly five o'clock by now, dark and cold. Aubrey would be worried, wondering where I'd got to. We still had no phone at the cottage. I wished I'd thought to ring the farm while I was at the pub, but it hadn't occurred to me that the weather would clamp down this much. Driving along with dipped lights lost in the swirls of snow, I was comforted to see Roger's headlights in my mirror. The main road, though not a very busy one, had been kept fairly clear by the traffic so I was able to make the final small hill without any problems. As I turned for Througham, I heard Roger hoot a farewell as he stayed on the main road.

"Oh Flops, we're on our own now. Let's hope we make it." If anything was going to cause me a problem it would be this road, but at least I could walk home from here if I got stuck. As Roger had predicted the wind had blown the snow into drifts at every gap in the hedge, driving it across the road. No one had driven along this stretch for some time and later I was to discover that no one else made it for the next three days, but at that moment I was concentrating hard. I was also praising the pickup for its bravery at taking the drifted mounds at considerable speed to ensure it kept going. I was prone to praising machinery when it obliged me because it always took me by surprise. Florrie was taking it all in good part, like a small child enjoying the times we seemed air bound over the larger drifts.

Putting my foot harder on the accelerator, I approached the final little uphill slope. The impetus of the truck sailed me on to the cottage, where Aubrey had left the five-bar gate wide open for me. He was standing in the front porch looking concerned as I slid the truck into the drive, managing to stop just short of the hedge. He shut the gate behind me.

"Why didn't you come home earlier? It's been snowing hard here for at least two hours," he asked, wrapping his arms round me in a crushing hug.

"It wasn't snowing much at Laura's. In fact, I felt a bit of a cheat saying I was coming home before three, but the few flakes were so big I thought it could be worse here" I began to describe my escapade and peel off my outer layers as we went inside. Aubrey guided me through to the sitting room.

"Oh wonderful, you've got a super fire going," I said, warming my hands. "They had a great fire at the pub and had all been drinking for hours so couldn't see any urgency in rescuing me. The little windows were so steamed up, it wasn't till someone looked out of the door they realised how hard it was snowing. Roger, who farms in Stroud, was great. He gave me a pull out and followed me all the way to the turning. He warned me there would be drifts. So much snow has blown through that big gap in the hedge in Upper Througham I didn't think I'd get through. The truck was great, but I never want to do it again."

I admitted that deep down I was terrified.

"I was fairly worried about you," Aubrey drew me to him again and squeezed me, another big bear hug.

Back in the kitchen while I put some supper together, Aubrey fed the cats. Florrie was still finding snow the most exciting thing ever and eventually came into the house with hundreds of ice balls attached to his legs, melting all over the kitchen floor.

Not only did I have Sunday off, but Monday and Tuesday as well. The snow fell for many hours through Saturday night and Sunday morning was magical. Everything was quiet. Silence in white. Drifts made the road impassable, but tobogganing was on.

Bleak but beautiful: that snowfall blocked the gateway into the field (top), and cut us off from the outside world until the snowplough could get through

CHAPTER 7

A Little Help From My Friends

When we started sheep farming, Aub was working full time for the Miserden Estate, so it was usually down to me and the vet to sort things out, and things went fairly smoothly, although occasionally we could have done with some help.

One Sunday morning, though, about seven o'clock our vet Rod found he also had Aub as an assistant, closely followed by our son Mark, returning home from a party. Rod was here to perform a caesarean and it would be useful to have a bit of muscle to lift the ewe onto the makeshift operating table.

Then the phone rang just as Aub had secured her legs to stop her kicking anyone. He was wanted on the Estate so offered his apologies and left. Mark took over while Rod prepared the ewe. After the first incision Mark turned a pale green and disappeared behind the shed to be sick. A caesarean and excess alcohol didn't mix.

Rod raised his eyebrows at me and smiled. "Same as normal then. You and me."

We both laughed and he carried on.

On another occasion our friend Martin, who culls the deer and foxes, called into the sheep shed to introduce a shooting friend he'd brought with him. Both helped to steady the ewe, who was finding it a little difficult to balance on a block of four small bales covered with a plastic sheet. No mean feat in any circumstances, but with her back feet tied together, even more of a challenge. She had to be brought to a height for Rod to operate and was in no discomfort.

As usual, I stood by to take the lambs as Rod cut the membrane and handed them to me. I took the first and dried it off with a towel, making sure it was breathing. As Rod indicated the second one was ready Martin's friend asked if he could rub it dry, and as it was obviously a goer, I accepted his offer, and carried on rubbing the first.

Martin continued to hold the ewe as Rod did the intricate stitching, both deep in discussion about deer numbers and the need to cull to maintain a healthy population. When all was done, ewe and lambs established in a pen with mother licking both her lambs, the shooting party moved off to their planned assignment.

The following weekend Martin's friend brought his family to see the ewe 'he'd lambed'– by then she was running around the field.

Later, my friend and neighbour Mary became my regular assistant. While she was helping, she asked if someone she knew could come to the farm during lambing.

"I know it's a pain, but I told her I'd been helping you with lambing and she's desperate to come up and see the lambs."

"No problem. We're through the worst of it, aren't we? Just tell her to wear something old and waterproof. If it rains again overnight, the yards will be like oxtail soup."

Mary and I had a complete wardrobe of warm, waterproof clothing, most well-worn, some acquired from charity shops and often looked like refugees, so it came as a slight surprise to see Angela disembark from her car in brand new, breathable waterproofs and spotless wellies straight from their box. I suggested that Mary showed her the latest lambs still in pens or small sheds then took her to have a look round the fields, as she fed outside. I was aware a young ewe was in the process of lambing, but she hadn't been on for long so I was leaving her time to open up and do some of the work herself before further investigation.

Mary took Angela on a fairly exhilarating ride on the quad, judging by Angela's hairstyle when she returned, at which point I managed to catch the young ewe, slipped her gently onto her side and asked Mary to hold her while I checked on progress. It was a big single lamb and a small ewe. While I worked at opening her up, with ample use of slipjel, I attempted to give a running commentary for Angela, standing in the walk-through feeder watching avidly. Gradually I was able to open the ewe sufficiently to feel the head and two feet. I managed to slip the plastic covered lambing wire inside her, up and hopefully over both the lamb's ears, then once fairly certain this would hold, started to extricate one of its huge feet. Securing this with a soft lambing rope I suddenly had a bright idea.

"Angela, could you just climb in here and hold this rope for me?" Delighted to be a part of the operation, Angela sat beside me, keeping the lambing rope taut while I ensured the wire was still in place and tied the other end of the lambing rope round the second foot. With Mary holding the ewe still, assuring her she would soon have her baby, I gently manoeuvred the feet and legs, drawing one a little ahead of the other to allow more room. Tying in with the ewe's contractions, applying gentle but firm pressure on ropes and wire, Angela pulled as instructed, then relaxed. Eventually timed with the ewe's final push, she ejected the front half of a beautiful white lamb, gradually allowing the rest to slip out. Quickly removing the wire and ropes, I passed the lamb round to her mother who welcomed her with joy.

"Well done everyone. Lovely ewe lamb." We all stood up and withdrew from the pen, allowing the ewe to happily lick her child. "Coffee. Must be coffee time."

Later that day, when Angela had gone, we were looking in the individual pen where the ewe and lamb were now housed.

"Better call her Angela, hadn't I?" We both laughed but the name stuck and the following year 'Angela' was a member of our Three Counties show team. The greatest surprise came a couple of weeks later, when we opened the Stroud News and Journal and found an article about Angela (the person) going into great detail about lambing her flock of sheep.

CHAPTER 8

A Classy Event Horse

I was thoroughly committed to Aubrey's dream of farming sheep, but I was encouraged to believe I should build on my personal aspiration of spotting and buying young horses when Laura's daughter Beth was searching adverts for 'a top-class showjumper/ eventer'.

The desire I had to produce and sell on young horses may well have come from the early days in my riding life when I worked in a dealer's yard. Horses and ponies came to us with very little education, often looking scruffy and unloved. While we rarely kept a horse for more than a month, it was amazing how we could change both its appearance and outlook on life in such a short time. Even before that time, while at Pat's, I had bought a four year old by her stallion, Palo, out of one of her Welsh pony mares; broke him in and sold him for a profit, then bought myself another. The real challenge was suiting the animal to the right home and rider, and I always felt great satisfaction when I managed to do this.

It was, however, still a dream to make my passion for producing horses a viable part of mine and Aubrey's plans to run our own farm. Then, one day during the summer holidays, Laura and I watched her daughter jump the winning round for the Cotswold team at the Beaufort's one day event. Beth was elated, but both Laura and I could see Smokey was struggling with the size of the fences.

"He's seventeen now," said Laura, stroking the grey's neck, as Beth went into the marquee for the prizegiving. "I hope we have him for another ten years, but Beth does need a younger horse. What we really need a 15.2 quality sort that's been there and done it with someone else. Keep your eyes open for anything in the Pony Club that's being outgrown. Beth keeps looking in *Horse and Hound* but I'd like to find something I know the history of."

The summer holidays soon came to an end with Beth no closer to finding a new mount. I thought I might have found something suitable and was about to mention it when Beth found her ideal horse advertised in *Horse and Hound*.

It was a grey and miserable day. We were en route for Maidenhead, listening to Beth raving about the horse we were going to see, who was going to take her to Badminton.

"Mum! He's a half brother to Harvey Smith's Johnny Walker. He's gorgeous, just the type I want."

"This is our exit, then first off at the roundabout. Did they say how much competition work he's done?" I asked.

"Not really, just kept saying we must come and see him because he'd be ideal," said Laura. "What a filthy day."

She'd almost run out of windscreen washer.

From the drive, we could see some show jumps in a small

paddock to the rear of a bungalow. Laura parked by the front door and we emerged from the car, relieved it had at last stopped raining. A tall grey-haired man came out of the house to greet us.

"Hello, hello. John Cavendish. You must be Mrs Edwards. Lovely, lovely to meet you." He pumped Laura's hand up and down as if to draw water, ignored me then turned towards Beth saying, "and you must be Beth, who's looking at our young show jumper. Come, I'll take you to the yard and introduce you to Adam, our work rider."

He led us around the bungalow to a small stable yard adjacent to the paddock. Three horses' heads were looking over the doors, two classical thoroughbred type bays and a very plain hogged chestnut.

"Oh my god, don't say it's the chestnut," Beth said in a loud stage whisper to me. "Oh please no."

"Don't be so silly," I said. "You said the advert said classy, and he's definitely not classy. It must be one of the bays. They both look the right type."

We were introduced to Adam, a lean young man, over six-foot-tall with legs up to his armpits, who in turn introduced us to Whiskey, the chestnut horse.

"This is the boy," he said. Unaware of the chill that had suddenly run through the air, he proceeded to put a head collar on the horse and lead him out of the stable, standing him up for his audience.

"Nice sort isn't he," John Cavendish stated rather than asked.

Beth looked about to burst into tears and Laura had lost

the power of speech so I quietly agreed that he looked a useful sort of cob, but not really what we'd been expecting.

"Your advert said he was a half-brother to Harvey's Johnny Walker. If I'm honest he doesn't look a lot like him," I said.

Beth was besotted by Harvey's iron grey thoroughbred.

"Yes, he's by the same stallion, just out of a heavier mare. But don't be put off. You see him jump. He's just like his brother."

As we'd travelled so far, Laura suggested we saw him pop round some fences and perhaps I could have a sit on him.

"I'm not having this," Beth assured her mother, "I'm not, Mum."

But Laura was adamant that it wouldn't hurt for Beth to see how he jumped. I was looking forward to seeing if this well-built cob could actually leave the ground.

Adam tacked him up, put on a pair of spurs and picking up a long schooling whip eventually persuaded the horse to trot into the schooling paddock. Whiskey was not looking at all enthusiastic. Glancing sideways I smiled at Beth.

"Don't worry, there's no way your mother's going to buy this. It's her warped sense of humour, making us watch it perform."

Ridden into a canter, with Adam's long legs wrapped round him like nutcrackers and the additional impact of the spurs, Whiskey headed for the first fence, a two foot upright of black and white rails. Slowing on the approach, once the schooling whip was introduced, he regained sufficient impetus to take off over it. His gait was such that he appeared to be trotting in front while his back legs were in canter, which did little to improve his ability as he scrambled over two more fences.

Laura, obviously enjoying the situation, played along with her part.

"That's great, now can we see him jump something more substantial? I'd like to be sure he could jump a Foxhunter course or do a novice event."

"He's not done that much," Adam started to say.

John Cavendish took over, assuring Laura that larger fences were fine. Adam, obviously aware of the horse's shortcomings, only raised the fences a few inches then suggested Beth might like to try him.

"Oh, I don't think Beth could, but it would be lovely to see how Sue gets on with him," said Laura sweetly. I glared at her.

"Yes, should've suggested that. Adam doesn't really get on with the horse, but I bet your young lady here will fly round on him," said Mr Cavendish nodding sagely.

"He's not what we're looking for, is he?" I started to argue but I knew that glint in Laura's eye.

She was going to have her way, at anyone's expense. Having driven all this way to look at something nothing like its advert, she was going to make the best of it.

Once mounted, my stirrups adjusted and whip in hand, (I'd suggested borrowing Adam's spurs but John Cavendish assured me, a good rider really wouldn't need them), I closed my legs on the cob and felt no surprise at the lack of response. After a couple of hefty kicks in the ribs, something I couldn't remember last doing, Whiskey did agree to move off and eventually face the first fence at his trot canter amble, which gave a most disconcerting feeling. I was pleased to be presenting him with a small obstacle and quite relieved when we reached the other side. To entertain Laura, I managed to hustle the horse over a couple more small fences before patting him on the neck and riding back to my audience.

"Don't think jumping's really his thing, do you?" I asked the open question as I slipped off the saddle and loosened his girth.

"He's definitely bred for the job," said John Cavendish. "He usually goes far better than that."

I raised an eyebrow, in no way feeling the fault lay with my riding.

"Of course he is," agreed Laura. "Could we just see his breeding papers? It would be great just to confirm everything." She implied we were still interested which brought a distraught squeak from her daughter.

"What are the two bay horses?" Beth asked. "Are they for sale?"

"Oh goodness no, they're my daughter's. Actually, I don't have his papers to hand, but I was assured of his breeding by the man I bought him from and have no reason to doubt him."

"Of course not," said Laura, gathering everyone back into the car. "I think we have a lot to discuss on the way home, but if we decide to buy, we'll be in touch. Goodbye, and please thank Adam for us."

In stunned silence we drove away, until Laura could contain herself no longer and burst out laughing. "We did pass a services didn't we? I must refill the windscreen washer and we'll get a coffee, though something stronger would be more appropriate."

"Mum, how could you? I almost believed you were interested in him."

"You toad, Laura," I said, with a broad grin. "You made that ghastly man's day, pretending you might be interested in that animal and risked a complete tantrum from Beth."

"I know. Well done, Beth. Obviously, I'm not going to buy you a cross between a carthorse and a mule. I just thought I'd make him put the horse through its 'so called' paces. Not to mention petrol, we've wasted half a day, so why shouldn't he?"

"Yeah, and what about my paces," I asked. "I've never ridden anything so uncomfortable in my life. Then I get the scathing remark implying I can't ride. Next time you like the sound of a horse, Beth; please discuss with me first. Better still, I may know where there's one you'll like. There's the services. Coffee's the best idea you've had yet, Laura."

I didn't need to call on my latent experience in horse dealing to know that there was never any chance that Whiskey was going to suit Beth, but finding something ideal for her produced unexpected results. It did more than give a teenage girl her new partnership. It also marked the moment when I truly began to understand my own dreams.

Finding Beth's ideal horse took a bit of doing because I knew how desperately she wanted to event at a higher level, but also appreciated her mother's financial limits. I'd first spotted the six-year-old at one of the events during the summer. A dark bay Irish thoroughbred cross. He was right at the top of Laura's budget, but had hunted a season in Ireland and one here. Jumping Newcomers, he'd won about sixty pounds and been placed in three riding club events. Having made contact with the owner, I arranged to see and ride him before suggesting Laura took Beth to try him. I was fairly confident he would suit her, but Beth fell in love with him immediately and Laura, still wincing at his price, acknowledged he was worth every penny.

I remembered then that I have always felt tremendous pleasure in producing horses. It encouraged me to build on this passion through future jobs, and then with my own horses when I dared to become a breeder. Looking back now, there are possibly some that I should have kept for myself, but often couldn't afford to turn down the prices I was offered. And there was always another challenge around the corner.

Showjumping

*Heather feeding the lambs with younger
brother Mark supervising from his pram.
Florrie is just visible behind*

CHAPTER 9

A Family of Three

Horses were definitely the catalyst behind our decision to have a family. There's never an ideal time during the farming calendar to have children, but to be honest, I hadn't really thought about it until someone buying a horse from me explained her reasoning. She was passing her older horse on to her husband to ride and wanted to buy herself a more challenging youngster.

'We've decided to have horses instead of children. I mean, I'm thirty-five now; who wants a temperamental fifteen-year-old around when you're fifty?'

I mulled this statement over for several days afterwards. Ok, so I was only 27, and as this was the seventies, I was termed an 'older mother' when I produced Heather at just 29, but it hadn't occurred to me to think forward like that before.

Aubrey and I had been married for four years, and thoroughly enjoyed the freedom we gave each other. I rode horses every day, competing most weekends, while Aub played motorcycle football or scrambled when possible. If one of us wasn't competing, we'd watch the other. Although we took the challenge of attempting to be sheep farmers seriously, we both had jobs we thoroughly enjoyed and the rest of the time just had fun.

Both our mothers had commented about pram designs and babywear, but we'd ignored these. Until now. Other friends in Througham had young children, perhaps it was time to think about it.

Precautions abandoned, I was soon discussing with our doctor how long I could carry on riding. Heather would be due in the middle of June, so he suggested I didn't actually compete in the Grand National, but apart from that to continue as normal while I felt comfortable.

I hunted up to Christmas and rode through to March. Bending over lambing pens was more difficult than usual and back in the late seventies we had no idea that abortion could be passed from sheep to women, although at six months pregnant I was probably past the danger point by then.

Obviously fairly fit and healthy, having Heather was not the easiest thing I've ever done. After spending a number of hours at Stroud hospital, on my own as it was during haymaking, it was decided there were complications and they had better facilities at Gloucester. This involved an emergency night-time ride in an ambulance, quite a drama, but eventually resulting in the birth of our lovely daughter. Aubrey did arrive at some point, a bit put out that having taken me to Stroud he then had to drive to Gloucester, and assured the nurse he definitely didn't want to be at the birth. He'd seen enough lambings and calvings ...

Home life with a young baby was daunting. While I'd read

plenty of books on lambing and rearing sheep, I hadn't really taken on board how testing it was looking after a baby, but gradually things fell into place. Luckily Heather was a very easy baby to care for. Living in Througham, with other young mums, I was offered lots of advice and help. Mary, just having had her second child, was a fount of wisdom and close at hand.

Heather, then later Mark, had to fit in with our lifestyle. Although we had bought a second-hand convertible pram, useful as a carry cot to lay on the back seat of the car, with wheels I could transport separately, I was delighted when Fiona lent me a wonderful old Silver Cross pram she had used for her own daughter. This had huge wheels, was beautifully sprung and was definitely the Rolls Royce of prams in its era. Heather would immediately fall asleep when pushed in this wonderful carriage, enabling me to park her in the field while I checked the sheep.

In the quiet backwater of Througham, a small entourage could often be seen travelling along the lane. Both our dogs Florrie and Annie walking alongside the pram and our two cats skipping along the coping stones of the wall, well out of harm's way but definitely supervising.

Heather was only six months old when Aubrey changed jobs and we moved to Bampton, in Oxfordshire. While Aub assisted Bill with the 2500 sheep on the farm, I was employed to look after four hunters. Luckily Bill's lovely wife Barbara had happily agreed to look after Heather in the mornings, so I could exercise the hunters, and had her for most of the day when I was hunting.

One afternoon when I was grooming the horses, I became aware of strange blowing noises coming from Lofty's stable. I'd just groomed him, but went back in to check all was well, only to realise I'd left Heather in his manger, a suitable place to put her while I groomed him, only this time I'd forgotten to move her to the next stable. Dear Lofty was just checking her out and Heather was perfectly happy with his warm breath, her tiny hands caressing his soft nose. Mental note to self, take baby with you.

Heather thrived that winter, never having coughs or colds and thoroughly enjoying life. The following spring we moved back to the Cotswolds, when Aubrey took the job as tractor driver at Miserden. Living in a lovely stone cottage at the far end of the village, we made new friends and found other young families with small children to play with.

Very soon a few more sheep gradually progressed into a small flock again. This time I was the one doing the day to day checks, and we had small parcels of land spread over quite an area. Checking sheep involved securing Heather in the back of our newly purchased but elderly Maxi, with Annie, our collie, loaded in the far back before I made sure I had everything I would need in the way of sprays and antibiotics for the trip. Then we would drive round to the numerous little fields, with Heather who was a toddler by now and Annie then running through the sheep while I tried to assess all was well. Attempting anything technical such as feet trimming or worming had to wait for Aub at weekends.

One trip Heather and I were sent on was to take a ram

to Gloucester market. With Heather secured in her car seat in the back of the Maxi, Aub helped to load the Suffolk ram in the small rear compartment of the car. All was fine, until the ram caught sight of some ewes just as we were leaving the field. Trying to turn round, he broke the catch that held the back seat up, separating him from the rest of the car.

"You'll be fine," Aub assured me. "Just get going and he'll settled down."

I can still remember that journey. Through my mirror I could see that the ram was pushing against the back seat of the car, gradually trying to fold Heather up in her car seat. I drove faster than I should, just hoping the seat would hold out until I got to the market, a good nine miles away, without folding our daughter up completely. Luckily, there were no more sheep to distract the boy on the trip and Heather gurgled and laughed all the way, the additional movement of the seat causing great hilarity. I was just relieved when I backed into an unloading bay and loosed the animal.

When I told Aub about our eventful trip he just said, "I told you it would be OK."

Heather and Mark – dressed in
the best 70s fashion

CHAPTER 10

And Another Makes Four

Heather's younger brother Mark was born when she was two. One child seemed quite easy, a second seemed like having six. Where Heather had sat quietly in horse's mangers and played with bits of tack, all Mark appeared to want to do was escape. His skill at climbing out of his cot at a very early age took us somewhat by surprise on an evening when friends were invited for supper. Having struggled to contain him while also trying to cook, Aub took over the childcare, announcing that he'd solved the problem. He'd found a spare cot side and tied it over the top, forming a cage. Miraculously, Mark stopped screaming and went to sleep, but different tactics were used the following night!

Checking sheep with two young children was challenging. Some ewes were grazing at Caudle Green, some five miles away from home, but at least I could park on the village green while I loaded one child into a front sling and the other on my back. By this time, of course, the dog had done two circuits of the field collecting the sheep, so greater dog training had to be added to the curriculum.

Summer months passed without too many disasters, but the winter of 1981-82 brought severe weather and heavy snowfalls. Earlier in January, Aubrey had been in charge of snow clearance, so I was able to drive to the farm buildings, where we were wintering the sheep, with little problem. However, as the severe weather progressed, he was involved with thawing out the milk-tankers who were having issues with their diesel freezing when they collected milk from Henley Farm.

The problem arose when the snowplough driver was taken ill and went home without telling anyone. Overnight the snowfall was so heavy it was impossible for a plough to move it the following morning, the pressure of snow likely to damage the stone walls. We were going to have to wait until a snow blower could be secured, or it thawed which didn't look likely in the next couple of weeks. For me, the problem was that the road from Miserden to Sudgrove, where we were renting a small barn, was over four foot deep with snow. I could cross the fields to get to the sheep, where the snow wasn't packed so hard, the wind having whipped up drifts that I could avoid, but with two small children it was a task too far. As usual in our village, help was at hand.

Mike and Sandra live on the corner by the pub and they agreed the best idea was to leave the children with them while I struggled up to feed the sheep.

I always hoped our children would be well behaved when left with others, and Mike, a wildlife artist, assured me that Heather settled down to drawing and painting at their sitting room table quite happily. Poor Sandra was later driven to visiting the pub next door for a schooner of sherry to calm her nerves after having Mark for a couple of hours. I gathered he spent most of the time trampolining on their Ercol settee and rolling their floor-length curtains round his body, like a mummy.

Sandra assures me the curtains are still there, so thankfully he didn't do them any lasting damage. Aren't we lucky to have such wonderful neighbours?

I never once regretted listening to the lady who bought my horse. Both children have been a source of entertainment from a very early age. Mike, who babysat in the snow, became Mark's best friend, walking through Miserden woods bird and animal spotting, both with binoculars around their necks. One wet February evening the local news mentioned it was ideal conditions for frogs mating, so Aub was dragged out by his enthusiastic young son to search for them. I gather they had wandered around the park, near the lakes, with no great success, until Aub made 'rivet rivet' frog noises himself, and they were greeted by a chorus from nearby frogs.

The resulting frogspawn led to one of Mark's first entrepreneurial successes. A sign appeared on our cottage gate indicating tadpoles for sale, different prices for different sizes. Several people paid for them, although they suggested Mark kept them safe for them until they changed into frogs.

Soon their school friends became regular visitors to the farm and proved willing assistants, returning home to amaze their parents with what they had done. Enthusiasm for lambing was really for staying overnight in the caravan, although both children can remember pulling their first lamb, Mark with excitement, Heather with disgust and a rapid washing of hands.

Very different our children. Both had their own sheep. Mark bred from his ewe each year and earnt around £400 annually from her lambs, aiding his finances right through uni. Heather sold hers back to us to buy a new coat!

One of my favourite memories of their childhood is how the summer shows were a delight. Having helped to scrub and clean the animals, they would show their own sheep and ours, sometimes the animals not really behaving as they should. They knew all the other Texel breeders and the pride in their eyes when they won a rosette made all the hard work worthwhile.

Now we enlist our grandchildren to help at lambing and sorting time. They fill buckets and hayracks, feed bottle lambs and operate gates in the sorting yard. What would we do without them? And their reward? They have the opportunity to visit the markets and the shows, and a market breakfast is the greatest prize of all.

CHAPTER 11

Children and Ponies

It was exciting to raise a young family on the edge of Miserden Park. A beautiful landscape of softly folding hills, surrounded by large areas of ancient woodland. Where the River Frome runs through the valley, it opens out into a series of reed-lined lakes, divided by mysterious woodland tracks and paths. Every part was an adventure.

When they were older, Heather and Mark used to play hide and seek with their friends in the hollow that surrounded Castle Tump, where the 12th century castle is thought to have stood, and later played cowboys and Indians there on their ponies. Overlooking the crossing of the River Frome, the castle appears to have guarded an important trade route going right up through the village, past Lypiatt Farm, where we now live.

Even when they were very small, we utilised the parkland as much as possible. The steep undulations of the fields did, however, mean that going down into the park was great fun for the children, running and playing; but the homeward journey was a little more testing. Ponies first became involved when I worked out it was easier to put both children on a pony for the uphill trip than push a buggy, a double one at that!

Heather's first pony Hobby, would often poddle back up the hill with his jockey fast asleep on his back. He was so careful she never fell off. We were then lucky enough to find Ella, a wonderful Shetland pony for Mark. Typical of this breed, she did have her quirks and could put in tiny bucks, usually if her jockey was doing something to annoy her. This was of no concern to Mark who just called it a back wheelie. We could often go for walks around the park and, probably having been talking to Heather, I'd turn to discover Mark had got off Ella way back to look at something interesting in the grass. It always reminded me of David Niven's comment about 'bring on the empty horses'.

While I usually bought myself a cheap young horse to produce, hoping to sell on for a profit, I always made sure the children's ponies were 100% safe. It's strange, but when you've ridden all sorts yourself and know how lucky you've been to escape major injury, you shield your children from the same possibilities. My parents had no idea of what I was doing and I rode many wild and difficult ponies in my youth, often because I was the only one brave enough, or possibly stupid enough, to get on them, but amazingly came away with few injuries. I must have learnt to either sit tight or fall well at an early age. During the school holidays, I insisted we rode each day. We would picnic by the ford, on the way to Caudle Green. Ponies could graze while Heather and Mark paddled in the icy water and if quiet enough, we often caught the highlights of gold and turquoise as Kingfishers darted around the water. At this point I was able to borrow something safe to escort them. As the summer progressed, Mark asked if we could ride first thing in the morning and I agreed that was a good time.

"I just meant then we can get it over with," he said.

Initially, Mark was quite brave on his ponies;, Heather was much more cautious. At one point she nearly lost her nerve altogether, until we found Charm, another Shetland. While looking for a larger pony for a friend, I had come across a lovely 12.2 hh grey gelding, Pebble, which I thought would suit Heather. He was totally safe, but his bucking displays in the field, when he decided he didn't want to be caught, had frightened her, even though he never put a foot wrong under saddle. While Ella was a miniature, standing only about 33 inches high, Charm was a full up 40-inch standard Shetland. Heather could look too big on her, but she was light and they had several great years together, including Pony Club camp.

We loaned Pebble to some friends; two competent riders and when they tried him was the only time I saw him buck under saddle, depositing the older girl. I think he looked after the less competent, but tested those with ability, reminiscent of Merrylegs in Black Beauty. They enjoyed him for two or three years then returned him for Mark.

Mark's competitive career was fairly non-existent. At one small gymkhana I do remember him insisting on eating a bag of crisps during a showing class, the judge simply pointing out that without the crisps he might ride quite well. He also decided he would do a small show-jumping class. To my dismay he wandered into the ring, pointed Pebble at the first fence which the genuine little pony popped over, then seemed to lose interest. However, Pebble then took it upon himself to negotiate the course and, to everyone's amazement, completed the round clear. Mark dismounted, handed me the pony and went off to get an ice cream.

Heather, at this point, was a little more competitive and she watched her brother in astonishment. However, I did decide maybe it was me doing the pushing when she came out of the ring on Smokey, a later pony, having had a refusal at the first fence. I was furious and tore her off a strip, telling her to use her legs. She went back in and jumped all the fences clear, including one made up of bales covered in black plastic, at which nearly every other pony had stopped.

"She was more frightened of you than that fence," another mother commented.

Perhaps it was time for a re-think.

Heather, competing with great determination

Leading Mark on Ella

CHAPTER 12

Becoming a writer

The first time I saw my writing in print was in *Cotswold Life* in 1980. I read and re-read my article for most of that week, my feet barely touching the ground. I'd organised Miserden Horse Show, and so I wrote a report about the highs and lows of the day for the magazine, and illustrated the piece with my pen and ink drawings.

This wasn't the first horse show I'd organised. As a teenager in Sussex, I'd run an annual village horse show, though this was less in the spirit of charity, as at Miserden, and I'd more of an entrepreneur – Initially, I'd purchased a showing jacket with the proceeds and the following year made enough to buy my first pony!

Writing was something I had always done, if initially simply scribbles in a notebook. It then became an important part of my life when Heather was small. Often on my own in the evenings, with Heather asleep and Aub working late, particularly during haymaking and harvest, I felt the need to communicate with adults, especially after a day spent talking to a two year old. This was when I first began writing about our somewhat eccentric lifestyle in Througham, and later our adventures into sheep farming.

My report about Miserden Horse Show for Cotswold Life magazine was a big step. It marked the moment that horses set me on a new career path of journalism. I was able to write knowledgeably about things I had done previously, such as showing and jumping and it also opened up other equestrian opportunities. I had also found a new income stream.

Soon after the publication of the first article *Cotswold Life* asked me to write about our farming experiences on a regular basis. I was delighted. This was followed by articles in *Farmer's Weekly* and then one in *Riding* magazine led to other opportunities with *Horse and Rider* and *Pony*.

These included the opportunity to interview soldiers of the Household Cavalry when doing a series on careers with horses. I visited the barracks about two months after the horrendous Hyde Park bombing in 1982, when a car bomb exploded, killing four soldiers and seven horses of the Blues & Royals while exercising in the park.

One seriously injured horse, Sefton, survived, but endured eight hours of surgery to remove shrapnel from 34 wounds. Quite understandably he became a British celebrity, featuring on television programmes, and was awarded the status of *Horse of the Year*. Thankfully he recovered sufficiently to return to active service until 1984, then living in happy retirement for a further nine years.

During Sefton's rehabilitation, I had an in depth interview with an extremely good looking Commander (or do all men always look handsome in uniform?). Then a guided tour of the new, two tier barracks to meet the lovely Sefton, well on his way to recovery. I was actually lucky to meet the real one – inundated with visits from the public who were distraught at the deaths and injuries to these lovely horses, Sefton proved so popular that look-alikes had to be placed in his stall throughout the day.

"If he'd eaten all the carrots brought for him, we'd have had a serious case of colic," the Commander told me, laughing. "Luckily, we have several horses with similar face markings, so they formed a rota!"

Looking back through my articles I appeared to have covered most equestrian fields. I wrote about almost every aspect of horsemanship, where I also gained new knowledge. I interviewed many top show jumpers and eventers with some heart-warming stories. Ian Stark talked of ringing home to say he'd won both the individual and team Silver medals at the Seoul Olympics, only to hear his daughter far more interested in telling him they had a new kitten.

He said, "After the excitement of top competition, it brings life into perspective."

At Badminton I often interviewed young riders on the Thursday and Friday, after their dressage tests, hoping for a first-time success and completion. Sadly, watching the screen in the press tent on the Saturday, I saw several I'd interviewed eliminated on the cross-country. It was back to square one for a story on Sunday.

A series on careers with horses saw me in major racing yards and studs, and another on showing gave me the opportunity to ride side-saddle, something I'd never experienced. When I asked to interview a well-known side-saddle rider, she immediately offered me a lesson.

"It's really the only way you'll be able to describe how it feels," she said, having ascertained that I could ride a horse.

Mounting from a block, Janet showed me how to place my right leg over the fixed pommel, with my right thigh lying across the saddle. My lower leg rested along the horse's near side shoulder. My left foot had a stirrup, the top of my left thigh resting just under the leaping head.

"See how your left knee is now secure. Sit up straight. Your shoulders must be back and level as if you're riding astride. Use the whip in your right hand as though it's your right leg. Now ask him to walk forward. How does that feel?"

"Yes, good I think." It was certainly different but within ten minutes I was walking, trotting and cantering confidently on both reins. Janet was right about my shoulders, once I dipped my left shoulder I felt completely out of balance. Very much like skiing, I was to discover later on, although riding side-saddle seemed an awful lot easier. As Janet had advised, there was no way my article would have been so detailed, had I not actually ridden.

I find that a lot of my life has been like that – my passion for horses, working alongside Aubrey with the sheep, raising the children – every new experience can lead to something unexpected, and greater fulfilment.

One year, Aub and the children came to Olympia with me, when I was working. Heather and Mark were thrilled to go behind the scenes, chatting to anyone and everyone. Heather recognised some of the riders and was excited to collect their autographs, whereas eight-year-old Mark collected autographs from anyone who would give him one. On the last train home he addressed most of the people in the railway carriage, asking for their autographs, and some he held in deep conversation. One gentleman, leaving the train at Swindon, turned to me and smiled.

"He knows all about my life now. Mind you, I know all about yours too." It appeared that Mark had been as forthcoming in relating tales of our family life as he had been in his enquiries of others.

CHAPTER 13

The Hunter Trials

Eventually, spring begins to awaken after the winter. First the snowdrops appear in the garden, under the laburnum tree, gracing the resting place of three of our much loved dogs. Then gradually the spring bulbs explode in a mass of colour, while the grass begins to show new green growth in the fields of ewes and lambs.

Spring also heralds the hunter trials and early horse shows. I had often competed at these events, but never really thought about their organisation, or how one becomes involved in them? It's very easy. You only have to murmur 'perhaps' to find yourself put down as judge for fence 12 for the next ten years. Several years ago, I found myself in this situation and was too slow to think of an excuse.

"I promised I'd help out ages ago," Jenny said. "Now James wants me to go with him to visit his aunt. I could just tell Pippa I can't make it, but it's so last minute – I just thought if I could find someone to take my place ..."

"I've never fence judged," I said, rather weakly.

"Oh, don't worry, it's only a small do, but really well

organised. You'll thoroughly enjoy it." Jenny was almost pleading at that point.

I should have been stronger. "Okay. What do I have to do?"

"It couldn't be easier. You all meet up at the judge's tent first and everything's explained. Then they give you your packed lunch and drive you off to your fence. You're not on your own, the TA will be close by doing the commentary and you usually get allocated your own dishy young soldier, so make the most of it!"

For the uninitiated, hunter trials are a cross-country competition, with varying degrees of difficulty. Most people will have watched the cross-country section at Badminton; well, a hunter trial is a much smaller version. Often held in the spring, timed with the children's Easter holidays, good weather is the norm, although, of course, on this occasion, it wasn't.

Sunday morning dawned, well, I supposed it had dawned – difficult to tell, it was so grey and overcast. At least it wasn't raining at that point. Well prepared with warm underclothes, thick socks in my wellies, gloves and woolly hat, topped with waterproofs. I did ask Aub if he'd like to come too, but he said he'd give it a miss!

I had two pens, in case one failed halfway through the day and at Jenny's suggestion, a hearty packed lunch and two flasks of coffee. Some venues treat their fence judges well, delivering a steady supply of food and hot drinks to the outlying posts during the day, not so at every event. Jenny told me that at one horse trial, they were issued with a pen and score sheet, no lunch, but half a bottle of wine each to take to their positions by the fences, which livened up proceedings considerably. I'd already decided that on a miserable day like today I'd definitely need something to eat and a warm drink.

As Jenny promised, there was a briefing in a small, crowded marquee. Gushingly welcomed by Pippa, the lady in charge, I was issued with score sheets then directed to the initiating meeting. Here the basics of refusals and disobediences etcetera were outlined and all fence judges were primed on emergency situations and introduced to their closest radio contact.

"Sadly, this year's event has coincided with our usual wonderful force of Territorial Army soldiers doing manoeuvres on Dartmoor, but they've generously sent some of the younger members to help out today."

I was introduced to a small pale faced blond boy.

"Now Harry this is Mrs …?" Pippa looked enquiringly at me.

"Oh, Sue, er Mrs Andrews," I said, aware that perhaps the organizers wanted them to address the judges more formally.

"Mrs Andrews. She will be at fence twelve and Mrs Derryman will be at eleven. You are stationed between them, Harry, so if they have a problem you can radio through for help. Remember, they will wave a red flag for a medical emergency and a yellow flag should their fence need attention. Is that clear with you, Harry?"

Harry nodded intently and tried to offer me a hand to shake. At that point both his hands were full with an awful lot of radio equipment, most of which he or I had to rescue on our way towards my fence and his outpost as he dropped it on the muddy woodland track. Lunches had materialized, but transport to our fences had not. This twelve-year-old didn't instil me with great confidence, should I have to call on his assistance in an emergency. So much for my promise of my own dishy TA soldier.

I felt almost unkind leaving Harry on his own, some way away from my fence, where he was able to see what was happening at the previous fence and mine. Clutching my lunch, score sheet and umbrella, I located fence twelve, a brush fence with a small ditch in front of it. That could cause a few problems, I thought, hoping I was just looking on the pessimistic side.

I settled myself in a relatively comfortable position on a convenient tree stump, using my thick scarf as a cushion. The rain had held off, leaving a chilling wind the competitors hoped would dry up the ground. Judging by the darkening skies the weather still looked as though it could turn a steady drizzle into a downpour any minute. I kept my umbrella close at hand. Sadly, I'd be unable to use the umbrella once the event began, the sight of one might frighten the horses. Hopefully it could keep my rucksack and sandwiches dry behind the tree.

Five minutes or so had gone by. I stood up and walked around close to my jump. I'd been told I would hear on the radio when the event started, but was slightly worried that I might not with young Harry in charge of the closest one. Should I wander up his way to check? If I did, the first competitor would surely come galloping down the track without me at my post. I clapped my hands to warm them; relieved Aub had suggested my fingerless gloves as well as the thick sheepskin ones I was wearing at the moment. Naked hands once I needed to write down the scores, was a daunting thought.

I'd checked my watch when I first stood up; another five minutes had passed when I ran down the path towards the little huddle hiding in a large bush some 100 yards from my tree stump. Difficult to distinguish, it had to be Harry. As I came closer a small fair head and pale face looked up in my direction, a tentative smile just turning the corners of his mouth. He stood up briskly, knocking a vital part of his radio equipment to the ground and was still grovelling in the leaves and mud to retrieve the final loose pieces when I reached him.

"Hello Mrs Andrews. Um, are you OK?" he asked apprehensively.

"Harry, wasn't the first class meant to start at ten? Have you got the radio set up okay?"

"Oh yes," he beamed at me. "I've tested it as well. I just haven't heard anything come through yet. The lady at eleven seemed alright, I just thought they're running late."

I glanced down the ride and the judge at eleven did seem content. Looking up at that moment and catching sight of us, she waved and shouted something that could be interpreted as 'these damned things never run to time'.

Comforted by her obvious calm, I agreed with Harry that that was probably the case, just as his radio crackled into life, proclaiming the start of the event and the first competitor was approaching fence one. I smiled at Harry and quickly retreated. He was a sweet boy, more under control than I'd given him credit for and felt a little guilty. No time to dwell on it as competitor number one loomed into view and sailed over my fence.

By now steady drizzle was becoming quite a dampening rain. Glancing wistfully at my umbrella covering my rucksack, I decided to put on the scarf to stop the rain dripping from my hat down my neck and elected to lean against a tree rather than sit again. Oh, why hadn't Jenny suggested bringing a chair? Why hadn't I thought of it?

As the morning progressed, more and more competitors appeared; some smiling, some gritting their teeth. Some came at such speed I wondered the pony had time to fold up his undercarriage and take off at the jump. Others with so little enthusiasm I knew they had no intention of attempting the obstacle, often seeming more inclined to run me over as they went round it. The experts considered my jump to be pathetic while smaller competitors were in awe of the fence, and stood more chance of falling off while praising their pony's brilliance at having cleared it, than they did actually jumping it.

Then came the competitor whose mount was putting on the brakes a good ten yards before the fence, but was eventually cajoled into facing it after doing some nifty footwork to the right and then back to the left for what seemed like forever, before eventually leaving the ground. Needless to say, he took the top half out with his knees, leaving a gaping hole in the centre of the jump, which was not classed as one that was designed to be knocked down. To my surprise on landing the rider turned around in the saddle to address me, as her horse continued at full gallop and strains of "that wasn't a refusal, he didn't step back" could be heard disappearing into the distance. This was backed up a few seconds later by an out of breath mother, assuring me that it wasn't a refusal as he hadn't stepped back or turned a circle.

The horse may not have stepped back and he didn't turn a circle, but my understanding of the earlier briefing led me to believe what he had done was classed as 'disobedience'. I made an explanatory note on the score sheet, hoping someone would understand, but couldn't ponder for too long as more important matters such as repairs to my fence had to be arranged. Waving my yellow flag, I alerted Harry, who radioed the situation through and halted further competitors; but not before the next one galloped through smiling, relieved to find the fence at half its original height.

Time for a quick cup of coffee and a sandwich while fence repairs were undertaken, then competitors started to appear again. I soon decided manners had gone completely out of the window on the cross country. As I caught a loose horse whose rider had parted company with it, satisfied myself the girl was alright then helped her on again, I was amazed to receive the screamed challenge of "can't you hold him still?" rather than a Thank You. Another rider appalled me by hitting the animal two or three times because he slipped coming into the fence and stopped, having found himself in an impossible position to take off. The ground was by now becoming very slick. I hoped the horse would find some suitable way to repay that treatment further along the course.

Out of the gloom, a small child riding a hairy pony with nostrils like red caverns and a mist of sweat mixed with drizzle arrived to collect my judging sheets. Giving me a dazzling smile, she stuffed the paperwork into her satchel and thanked me, before galloping on to the next fence.

There followed quite a long gap in the proceedings before another horse and rider appeared, thankfully time for another coffee. Was this still Class 1 or were they now on to Class 2? No information was emitting from Harry's department, not even a crackle. Radio communication seemed to have broken down. Even the next rider wasn't sure which class he was in, just that it was the novice class. Aren't they all, I wondered? Hearing the call for first aid to one of the later fences I wondered if the poor horse that had been blamed for his refusal had finally dealt with his rider.

Eventually the radio emitted a loud crackling sound which indicated the end of the event. Gathering up my belongings I trudged wearily back to the briefing tent. Harry waved a tentative hand in farewell as I looked in his direction en route. I was happy to see a landrover had come to collect him and all his miscellaneous equipment, which I felt would have been a struggle to get back in one piece.

While scores from the earlier classes had already been collected by the assortment of children riding 'Thelwell' type ponies, going faster than most of the competitors, I found Pippa and handed in the final score sheets. Graciously accepting Pippa's thanks for 'being such a stalwart' and flinching slightly when she said she would be in touch with both Jenny and me before next year's event, I suddenly became aware of the shrill cries of a female voice demanding to see the judge from fence 12 because she had already explained to her that it was not a refusal. With more speed than dignity I beat a hasty retreat for the car park.

"Just you wait 'til I see you, Jenny," I muttered as I climbed into the driver's seat, relieved to know I would soon feel warm and comfortable for the first time that day.

Dishy TA, lovely lunch, great fun. Who did you think you were kidding?

Chapter 14

Charollais Incident

As lambing progresses, tempers become shorter. Conversations are only carried out if deemed necessary and unavoidable, and then only in short, sharp, succinct sentences – particularly when you'd had an accident and are lying in agony on the ground.

"I don't know why you were in the pen in the first place," Aub said, as I lay there, groaning. I thought it was quite obvious why – he'd said he needed my assistance.

We were tagging the two remaining lambs on the Charollais/ Texel cross ewe, the third having been adopted onto a ewe with a single. When the Charollais had given birth, another ewe had tried to steal her babies, and having three took a bit of keeping up together so we'd rearranged things a little. She was also as wild as a coot, so we'd penned her in the corner of the sheep shed, rather than taking her to the main lambing pens. This was why she was in an odd shaped pen, longer than usual, to fit the hurdle size. One of the problems.

While Aub was still sorting out the tags and fitting them in the pliers, I attempted to be helpful and spray the blue number on the ewe's side. Ewe's with twins have blue numbers, singles red, so we know if a ewe with a blue number has only one lamb, she's misplaced one.

Having checked the first lamb's tag I managed to spray a reasonably recognisable number on one side of the ewe, but when I suggested she turned round for me to do the same on the other side she charged forward, straight between my legs, carrying me forward at speed, a greater distance than she could have covered in a normal pen, until the metal RSJ at the corner stopped my flow. The impact on the RSJ should have been painful, but compared to the agony of the wrench she'd given to my thigh, it paled into insignificance. I leant against the hurdle at the back of the pen, moaning in tears.

"Get my leg off her," I shouted, still riding her astride, backwards. Aub managed this. "I think I need to lie down."

He undid the hurdle and let me through to the next large pen where I collapsed in the straw.

"You alright?"

How do you answer that? I'm writhing in agony, lying face down on not the cleanest of straw beds, but soon realise he's furious at the inconvenience.

"I've pulled my leg muscle. It really hurts. You carry on, I'll just lie here."

Perhaps I didn't think he'd take me at my word. That there might be a little comfort or sympathy, but no, he simply proved he could tag and tail the lambs without my assistance, though he's always demanded it before. He could also fill in the paperwork and spray the number on the ewe without her maiming him. Then, to add insult to injury, he opened the back hurdle and let the ewe and her two lambs into the big pen where I was still lying face down in the straw, not daring to try and move. The pain was excruciating. Without a word he then moved off to the far end of the sheep shed to tag the other lambs, before disappearing to the grain store to tag the final two. Aub is so used to me being tough and hating a fuss, he thought he was doing the right thing.

After what seemed like an age, I tentatively moved my leg, only to wince with pain. I lay still again; though found I could move my body position slightly. Somehow I was going to have to get to the truck, as emergency services seemed sadly lacking. Gradually I found a way to stand up, although I can't say it was pain free. Holding on to the wooden struts at the side of the sheep shed I slowly and tentatively made my way to the front. The ewe, quietly eating at the hayrack, eyed me with suspicion and moved her children further away from me.

Opening the gate, I eventually, with the help of the metal gates along the front of the shed, managed to take miniscule steps towards the truck parked at the far end. I was almost there when a silver Mercedes drove into the yard and pulled alongside me. Was this a mirage? I'd been so unfair with my thoughts, Aub had obviously contacted someone to come and collect me. He hadn't just left me lying in the straw. A very smart elderly lady wound down the window.

"So sorry to bother you, but the postman has left a package with us at Waverley House when it's addressed to Warneford House. I can find Warneford Cottage but not Warneford House. Could you direct me?"

Of course. She thanked me after receiving directions,

turned her car in the gateway to the front field and steadily drove off again. This was surreal. I expect she thought all farming yokels had ashen, tear stained faces and were clutching a gate. Or even clutching at straws. Tottering on I managed to make it to the pickup and even more surprising got myself in and sat down. Even that was painful as there was a bruise on my backside where another of those bloody Charollais crosses had tripped me up on the concrete two days previously, and I suddenly became aware of the RSJ damage.

I managed to extricate my phone from my pocket and realised it was nearly half past twelve, so when Aub appeared around the corner I said he must bottle the lamb in the stable as I'd last fed it at 6.30 that morning. He bottled the lamb, topped up another and drove me home.

"Can you walk?" he asked, maybe wondering whether I was going to take up more of his time by needing help into the house. Although at this point he did think I was simply bruised.

"Yes, I think so." I shuffled off towards the house while he drove back to the farm to turn the newly tagged lambs and their mothers into bigger pens or out in the paddocks. I then discovered there was no way I could take my wellie off on the boot jack, so when he arrived home half an hour later, I was still wearing both my left boot and waterproof trousers, which were attached. Gently, though still painfully, Aub wiggled my foot in different directions and removed the boot and trousers. He was obviously a bit miffed I hadn't cooked his lunch while he'd been out, as he was meeting with a contractor at two. But he managed to cook beans on toast for us both and at my request even lit the fire before he left again. In fairness to Aub he is not unfeeling. We were both fairly exhausted at this point in lambing.

The only upside to my injury was I was totally grounded for the next four weeks. When I rang the doctor, he simply said, "Oh, hamstring. Just rest it. You'll be out of action for six weeks. Do you need a certificate?"

I wasn't sure who I would give it to, so declined.

Feeding the bottle lambs

CHAPTER 15

Bottle Lambs

I now have a scattering of old plastic garden chairs around the farm, usually kept for meetings and visitors, as I find it far easier to sit on one of these, rather than squatting down when trying to get a lamb to suck a bottle. Nothing to do with the hamstring injury, more with my age! Persuading a lamb to take even a third of a pint of milk from a bottle can take up to ten minutes, by which time I'd definitely have cramp in both legs and wonder if I'd ever get up again, hence the chair rather than doubled up on the floor.

Early on in lambing this is usually a case of topping up a lamb whose mother has not yet produced sufficient milk. In the latter part of lambing it's more likely to be one we've taken off a ewe because she has sore teats or even mastitis. Once I persuade it to take a bottle, its drinking technique gives an insight into why the ewe has become sore. Sometimes, these lambs suddenly grasp the correct way to suck, but more often than not they continue with their odd lack of skill.

The lambs which are taken from their mothers at a young age (when the ewe only produces milk on one side or has had three or four lambs to rear on two teats) quickly learn to suck a bottle teat. Then they begin feeding ad lib from the warm milk buckets before ending up on a bottle after five weeks, as if left longer on the ad lib system they gorge themselves and die.

If we have space I move the older lambs into stables, putting a hurdle across the doorway and bottle them with half a pint of milk three times a day on a bottle rack. This allows me to feed four lambs at a time for a further three weeks, along with weaner pellets and fresh water. It is amazing how much this improves the lambs. Then I wean them completely to dry food at eight weeks.

Even adding a fresh supply of lamb milk to the bucket is a skill on its own. With five or six lambs in together, at least one will put its feet in the bucket or stand on the lid like a circus elephant, while another will nip me with its sharp little teeth. I sometimes wonder why I'm bothering with them.

This May, I still had eleven lambs on bottles, all from the April lambing flock. Three of these had just come off the bucket, having reached that magic age of four and a half to five weeks, where their stomach gets the better of them. At this point they drink for England at one meal, bloat and die. Before now, I've been tired and hectic and then despaired when I missed the tell-tale signs. Sometimes I've even thought to check the age or simply remove the lamb to a bottle department, only to discover him dead when I next arrive at the farm. Not so this time. A Blue Texel was looking very full after I'd replenished the bucket so I immediately took him out of that department to prevent a second helping. On checking dates I realised all three of these final lambs would be better off on restricted feed.

Texels, Blue Texels and Charolais crosses are all greedy. They take bottles from the rack immediately, even though some milk runs out of the teats and onto their noses before they start sucking. Not so with Lleyns. Much smaller sheep, bred on the Lleyn peninsula in North wales, they are very suspicious of anything new – and milk falling on their noses is a definite no-no. In one stable I had three Lleyns and a Charollais cross. The Charollais immediately grabbed a teat with great enthusiasm, rocking the whole rack up and down, spreading milk everywhere. Obviously the three Lleyns couldn't possibly join in and disappeared to the other side of their pen at speed. Luckily, there was a Lleyn in another pen to swap over. The Charolais moved in with another crossbred and two Texels, all of whom were extremely bold with the bottles. Gradually all four Lleyns realised that it was suck a bottle on the rack or go without. Within a few days everyone was getting along fine.

I already had seven weaned lambs living in a section of the sheep shed. Once they came off the bottle, I moved them to different quarters as it gives them something else to think about, a distraction from the lack of milk. Three started as orphan lambs. The first two lost their mother to 'black bag' mastitis, the most severe and painful form of the disease, when they were only three weeks old. Fortunately, they rapidly took to the bottle, didn't lose condition in any way and now looked as big and striking as any lamb out with its mother.

Sadly, during the hottest April I can remember, we actually

lost a Blue Texel ewe from heat stress, so I moved the Blue lamb in with the other two. The two white lambs jumped around with excitement when bottles arrived, sucking with great enthusiasm. Initially, the Blue looked at me in horror when I offered him a bottle, thinking I was offering him a hand grenade, to be avoided at all costs. He really needed this milk, but trying to catch him felt as though I was wrestling with a hippo. Eventually he caught on.

Lambs are weaned off milk when they appear to be taking sufficient in feed pellets. The large pen in the sheep shed allows them plenty of room, ad lib pellets and fresh water and hay. After they've eaten some breakfast, I let them out into the field behind the buildings, to skip off, bounce around for a while, then settle to eating grass. If the dogs are with me, it can cause them some embarrassment. The lambs are intrigued by the dogs and want to investigate them. Sheepdogs don't talk to lambs. They command them. After some small confusion, all is on track again.

They come back in at lunchtime to eat more pellets and sleep in the shade. They know the system and are quite content. Eager to go out, but happy to come back in when I call them. As the younger ones join them, they simply follow guidance from their elders. While their final destiny is often the butchers, I certainly give them as happy a lifestyle as possible while they are with us.

Chapter 16

Miserden

History is everywhere in this village. It lives in the rows of stone cottages, the winding lanes that meet at the centre and, of course, in the great gabled manor house that gazes out over the wooded valley. I have always found this place captivating.

When we first married and moved to Miserden, the estate was managed by Wing Commander Sinclair, of the Royal Canadian Airforce, who married the widowed Mrs Margery Wills in 1943. She was a great source of information. It was quite by chance that I ended up meeting and talking with Mrs Sinclair as she was then called, but it must have been at the Park. She was a good age, and didn't venture out much, but was only too happy to reminisce. Some of her tales, like that of there being several inns in and around the village, are backed up by cellars in the cottages and mentions in history books, but her assurance that Edward the Black Prince once lived in the house may have been in her imagination, although his wife did inherit the property at one point.

Margery Sinclair was a great horticulturalist, the gardens well stocked with roses and peonies. Her favourite colour was pink and she was particularly fond of the pink cherry blossom trees the Wing Commander had planted for her, lining the main drive into Misarden Park from Winstone, and several also around the gates and lodge in Miserden, although sadly these are no longer there.

Of Scottish ancestry, she was also immensely proud of her herd of Ayrshire cows, that stemmed from two pedigree heifers she received as a gift in the 1950s. I could tell they had been very special to her. With the help of herdsman, Joe Teasdale, they built up a prize-winning herd of pedigree cattle, that were exhibited very successfully all over the country. Joe, then retired, was still living in one of the pretty gabled cottages in the village when we first moved here.

Many Cotswold towns and villages were built on proceeds from the wool trade in the middle ages, but I know that Miserden has been here since Saxon times. Appearing in the Domesday book as Greenhampstead, it was passed to the Musard family by William the Conqueror in about 1068. The village was named after them, eventually evolving to Miserden.

The estate has been in the ownership of numerous families and the crown since 1086, and perhaps that shows in the village's character. By the end of the 13th century Misarden Park was managed as a deer park with several lakes, recorded as fish ponds. In 1535, it is believed that Henry VIII and Anne Boleyn hunted in Misarden Park, while staying in Painswick on their honeymoon.

Henry VIII apparently wished to reward his comptroller of the King's household for arranging their excellent day's hunting. When asked what he'd like, Sir William Kingston said he'd have Miserden. Not a bad gift! At that time the village formed part of a marriage settlement for Henry's wives, but it was granted to the Kingston family after the death of Henry's last wife, Catherine Parr, so it appears the village did become Sir William's reward for a good day's sport.

While England was involved in many power struggles over the years, the community here moved quietly from medieval to Tudor times and onwards into the present with a farming tradition still at its core.

Many of the houses in the village carry names of previous owners of Miserden. In 1620, when the Pilgrim Fathers set sail for the New World, Misarden Park became the property of Sir William Sandys, and it was in Sandy's cottage, overlooking Horse Close, where Aub and I began married life and spent several happy years there.

In 1643, civil war brought 300 roundheads to garrison in the park. Lady Margaret Sandys, widow of Sir William, probably in her early sixties and a royalist, would have been less than pleased when forced to share her home with the other side during the struggles.

Sir John Rolt, whose initials can be seen above many of the cottages and the old village school, improved facilities in the village considerably and enlarged the holding. He added Wishanger Manor to the estate, rebuilt the school, and established allotments for estate tenants to grow their own food. Miserden appears to have been a happy and prosperous village for the majority of its history.

At the end of the 19th Century the estate was owned by

the Leatham family. This was a time of serious agricultural depression throughout the country, brought about by the supply of cheap corn and meat from North America and Australia. Again, Miserden was lucky to have owners with sufficient wealth to be able to continue to farm the estate, but it still changed things for the village. Needing to cut the workforce, some villagers were forced to find work elsewhere.

In 1911 Arthur W Leatham, son of the original purchaser, put the estate up for sale. The agents, Knight, Frank and Rutley said it was 'one of the most beautiful properties in England', the main house being described as 'an old stone built Elizabethan Mansion.' It included stabling for eleven horses, attractive pleasure gardens, a lake with boathouse, islands and trout fishing. However, it took two years before the property found a new buyer in the Wills family, part of the Imperial Tobacco Company, who own it today.

Another older member of the village who was a delight to talk to was May Holder. Then in her late eighties, I arranged to call on her as I felt she must have hidden gems to tell. Sitting comfortably in her garden, one sunny afternoon, one highlight she remembered was when the new wing of Miserden Park caught fire. A small child at the time, living at Church Farm, in the centre of the village, she recalled how she and her brother were told to stay in their beds while their parents rushed down to the park to form part of a bucket chain bringing water up from the lake.

"It was early in the morning, only just light. There was a lot of shouting, and men running down the road towards the

Park. The big house was on fire."

In 1914 an East Wing had been added to the house, providing a new billiard room and nursery, but in the early hours of a March morning in 1919 fire broke out in the new nursery. Fortunately one of the nurses woke in time to rescue the three children.

"The family had a Rolls Royce, but petrol rationing meant they had no fuel, so a man was sent the eight miles to Stroud on a bicycle to alert the fire brigade. Sitting up in bed, it was so exciting. We seemed to wait for ages, but eventually we could hear the fire engine approaching, horses at a gallop, as they reached the slight downwards turn in the road past our bedroom window, on the final run to the Park. Then we saw the fire engine, drawn by three huge grey horses."

Sadly, she added that it had taken so long for the fire service to reach Miserden, the horses unable to pull the engine faster than a walk up the steep hill from Stroud, that while the main house survived, the new wing was destroyed. This, however, was replaced the following year by one designed by Sir Edwin Lutyens.

In 1927 Frederick Noel Wills tragically died from peritonitis, a burst appendix. When his widow, Mrs Margery Sinclair, gave me her own account of the village's history, she explained with great sadness that he simply didn't reach hospital in time for doctors to operate. Miserden is by no means remote, but is about eight miles from the nearest town, being almost equidistant from Stroud, Cirencester, Cheltenham and Gloucester. Even today, I feel that distance whenever it snows or we need an emergency vet visit.

All the same, we are so lucky in this small community to have a village shop and post office where Jon and Laura supply all our needs and a village pub, The Carpenter's Arms, where Kev and Debs have been life savers. One Sunday evening, during lambing, I asked Aub if he'd like roast beef for supper.

He looked at me, totally amazed. "You've been in the sheep shed all day. When did you find time to cook today?"

"I didn't, but Debs did at the pub, and I'm picking up two plates of roast beef dinner on the way home."

Miserden Estate continued to flourish after the Second World War. When their tenants retired or died, the Sinclair's brought these properties back under their management, until only Clements Farm on the road to Whiteway was left tenanted. At one point the estate grew to over 3000 acres, including Jackbarrow, Stoney Hill and Birdlip.

When Aubrey went to work for Miserden Estate in 1978 he was one of sixteen tractor drivers. The farm had three dairies, over 1000 sheep, three foremen and a farm manager. A little later they started a pedigree Simmental herd of beef cattle. Farming enterprises on the estate have continued to change throughout its history and when Aub left in 2000, the estate had mainly reverted back to arable.

In 1980, when Mrs Sinclair died, the estate passed to her grandson, Major Tom Wills, who continued farming it, and expanding the forestry until passing it to his son Nicholas in 2016. It is still very much a family run, rural estate. The gardens are still beautifully maintained and open at certain times to the public, while the adjacent nursery flourishes, especially now with the addition of the Garden café.

Even on a smaller scale, this village shows its history. Many families have lived in this beautiful village, appreciating the countryside around them. While the estate as a whole continued to be based around agriculture, I have heard details of other small industries in and around the village. Workers were involved in the cloth industry; a carpenter and cabinet maker are recorded living here, as is a blacksmith, who would obviously have had plenty of work. There was even a collar maker and reports of both a butchers and bakers up to the early 1900s.

This small village has been such a hive of activity. Wouldn't it be great if the stone walls of the cottages could talk, or the sycamore tree in the heart of the village pass on memories of times gone by? There was apparently a major posting inn by Lypiatt Farm, where we now live, and many travellers would also have passed this way. Surely the horse drawn coaches that ran through the village must have left some ghosts.

Above: Heather, Mark and friends touring
Miserden village in a pony cart
Below: Aubrey with some of Miserden Estate's
machinery in the eighties

CHAPTER 17

Farming neighbours

Over the years I've found that support between farming neighbours is always given freely, even if it doesn't always take the form you expect. Early in our farming journey, we were given some rather difficult geese, and Aub suggested I visited his cousin Sally for advice. She kept two geese on her parent's farm some way into the next valley from Miserden.

By now, I knew Aubrey's family well and loved them dearly. His large collection of cousins had made me aware of the sibling fun I'd missed being an only child. However, I'd already had experience of the family's animals when one of Aubrey's uncles gave us our first ram. This sheep was called Satan, and his personality matched his name.

So, with that in mind, I was a little wary about visiting Sally at her family's farm on my own to ask about geese.

As it was, however, I soon realised that Aub and I were not the only ones having excitement with our livestock.

Sally's family consisted of parents Malcolm and Judy, her brother Joe, who was married and living in the next village, and her younger sisters Margaret and Lizzie. As a boy, Aub had lived in the same village, and spent a lot of his childhood at Harcombe Farm, his cousins being more like brothers and sisters. As I discovered long ago, Harcombe is a fun place to visit. Over the years there have been many pet animals on their farm, several of these normally termed as livestock! These included Sally's pride and joy – two beautiful white geese, and a gander, Walter, who terrified everyone, but adored Sally, following her everywhere. Another was Sophie, an elderly Suffolk cross ewe, who wandered in and out of the house at will, and a recent addition was Sucky Bunter, one of the dairy cows retired on the farm. When Lizzie – Sally's youngest sister, then aged nine – drew up a list of those privileged enough to enter the family nuclear shelter (should they happen to have one, and should the necessity arise in that climate of the Cold War), she'd included so many animals, there would be little or no room for humans.

When I arrived that summer's afternoon, I was greeted at the garden gate by her father, Malcolm, and the news that he'd begun a new farming enterprise. The clue was in his greeting:

"Good afternoon, good afternoon my dear girl, and how are you?" Malcolm was a burly gentleman, taller than me by some eight inches, with wild greying hair. He wrapped his arms around me in a suffocating bear hug and, not waiting for a reply, continued, "Did you know that Churchill once said *'the pig is a gay animal'*, in the old-fashioned way of course, very happy creatures, *'with a remarkable capacity for reproduction'*. Did you know that?"

Malcolm was prone to asking difficult questions. He

had left school at the tender age of 14, as had many farmers' sons during the war years. But over the next fifty years his love of literature and tireless study had earned him a degree at Cambridge, he was very well-travelled and could talk knowledgably on almost every subject. He quoted Shakespeare to his cows, and his favourite author was the Russian novelist Dostoevsky.

Reeling a little from the strength of his hug, I apologetically admitted that this particular quotation was not one I was conversant with. Malcolm wasn't waiting for my answer anyway. He led me into the barn to show me 50 eight-week-old gilts – young female pigs – he'd just purchased. The fact that Malcolm knew very little about pigs, other than 'Perky' a pig bought for his son when he was still at school, didn't concern him at all. In fact, if anything, it seemed to encourage him in his venture.

"No one is too old to learn, my dear girl, remember that, no one is too old to learn."

He guided me around the large pen, patting me heartily on the back to the point that my teeth rattled, then took me to the house for refreshments. Sally was curled up on the huge sofa in the large farmhouse kitchen, head in a magazine.

"Nice surprise," she said, looking up at me.

"It's you I've come to see, but your father side-tracked me to his new venture."

Sally rolled her eyes and groaned. "He gets madder by the minute. Just because life's improved now he's retired from milking, he thinks all is going to be perfect with the pigs. He knows nothing about pigs. Tea? Have a seat."

"Please. Your dad did say he didn't know anything about pigs."

"He doesn't have a clue. It wouldn't be a problem if he'd just bought weaners to fatten on and sell, because they can eat themselves stupid and grow, and he could've made money. But oh no, he wants to breed pigs. I mean, who starts something like that with as many as fifty? He's not sure whether to keep them indoors or out and knows nothing about farrowing. It'll be a disaster."

Malcolm thought life had taken a wonderful turn. No more rising at 5am to milk a herd of dairy cows, and all those lovely little pink squirmy things eating well and growing at speed as only pigs seem able, but I could see Sally's concerns.

"Anyway," I said, "I've come to ask you advice about geese."

I took my mug of tea to the sofa and we chatted for most of the afternoon, but it didn't take long to realise Sally's geese just lived happily on the farm without much of a problem.

It was several weeks before we had the second instalment of the Pig Saga. Apparently selecting an ideal husband for the gilts had proved to be anything but simple.

The first boar was called Brian.

"Wonder why?" laughed Aubrey when he heard, knowing the family had a mutual friend of that name.

We were told that Brian was a great big ugly thing of uncertain breeding, but at least he knew what to do. If the gilts wouldn't stand for him, he got quite vicious. After a couple of nips, they stood and he just got on with it. Trouble was, he was really lean to begin with, but with good food and good living on the farm, he put on so much weight he literally flattened the gilts. The family had to take him out before he killed them.

On our next visit we were introduced to the latest boar.

"Meet Boris," said Malcolm. "He's a Large White."

Of true aristocratic breeding, Boris was as gentle and handsome as Brian had been rough and ugly. So gentle in fact, that the ladies, all now expecting to be put in their place again, turned and attacked him. But unlike Brian, who had reasserted his position after a couple of snaps, Boris was taken aback by this unladylike behaviour and crawled into the corner, stuck his head under the water trough and lay there trembling. All this had happened when Malcolm, who was really far more interested in the arts than farming, had disappeared to Cambridge on a poetry weekend. The rest of the family, who were holding the fort rescued Boris, who was looking extremely unhappy.

We heard later that Margaret had to wrap him in blankets, bedded up to his eyeballs in straw under an infra-red lamp, before, eventually, she managed to feed, cosset and caress him back to life.

"I can imagine Margaret taking charge of the situation," said Aubrey. "But have they managed to get the gilts in pig?"

They hadn't. Now that it was clear that Boris was obviously inexperienced and frightened by the size of his harem, the receptive gilts were led to his pen one at a time, with someone standing guard to make sure he wasn't molested. This gradually rose to two gilts each day, until a vet happened to mention that even two a day was far too many pigs.

A young boar shouldn't have more than four a week!

Malcolm was horrified. I imagine he was looking around the building at the number of gilts still to serve and realising that it was going to be a very slow job.

The vet suggested he got another boar ...

Finally, the results of the amorous attentions from Brian, Boris and the new boar Dai became evident. We watched as the pigs grew fatter by the day and lounged around their quarters with contented smiles on their pink faces. Every time I visited, Malcolm could be seen strutting around the premises surveying the situation with equal contentment.

As the pigs neared their due time, excitement began to build. Malcolm announced he'd not felt so tense since England played Germany in the World Cup!

"Surely," I said to Sally, "things are easier for him now?"

They weren't. Malc had gone out to check the sows late one evening, the pigs being due to farrow fairly soon and was greeted by a hideous munching sound. The first sow had farrowed, killed her piglets and chewed them into little pieces. The shed was a battlefield with dismembered bodies lying all around this gore-covered sow, blood dribbling down her chin. I could imagine his and the family's horror. At that moment a herd of pigs could have changed hands for next to nothing. I remember thinking thank goodness that Aubrey and I had chosen to keep sheep – although we can have problems with our ewes when they lamb, they never present anything as gruesome as this.

Then things really began to happen. Within a few days there were pigs farrowing all over the place. As Malcolm was prone to recite poetry during a crisis, he described it to us later by relating it to *The Charge of the Light Brigade* – "There were pigs to the right of us, pigs to the left of us …"

But even then not all was going to plan. Apparently one sow had chosen to farrow among the calves, knocking down all the hurdles and demolishing about twenty bales of straw. Another knocked the door open and started producing her litter outside the barn. She'd opened the door, she had no idea how to close it, consequently others walked out and were found rooting up the winter barley.

Order resumed, sows and piglets were safely housed in pens, and thankfully no others were wishing to harm their children. Unfortunately, the excitement didn't end there either. The farrowing house was built on a low contour of the farm and one Sunday afternoon a few weeks later a thunderstorm struck with extreme ferocity. It was a Sunday, and Malcolm, a staunch Methodist, was changing to go to chapel when glancing out of the bedroom window, he saw the drain outside the farrowing house was awash, and water flooding inside. He shouted down to Margaret, who, with the urgency required, raced through the deluge to clear the drain and save the pigs.

It was just a shame that no one had accounted for Walter the Gander.

Malcolm watched from the window as Margaret was waylaid and chased down the road.

In the end, clad only in his shirt and underpants, Malcolm had to race to the yard himself, grabbing his wellies en route to clear the drain and open the doors to the farrowing house. He found that the sows were up to their middles in water, and the piglets, in true military tradition, had occupied the high ground.

"They'd taken over a small stack of bales in one corner. It just looked like a large pink mountain," Malc told us.

Everyone embarked on the rescue. What was most impressive was that, in spite of everything, Malcolm still managed to make it to Chapel on time.

I don't think Malc could face another year of pig breeding. The eventual outcome of the pig project, with all its dramas and trauma, was that most of the pigs found their way to Gloucester market and Malcolm and Judy visited Kentucky on the proceeds.

And for me and Aubrey – we found that we hadn't gleaned much useful advice about how to manage our difficult geese. But it certainly came as a relief to learn that sometimes other farmer's lives could be even more chaotic than ours.

Chapter 18

Leaps and Bounders

I met John when looking for some grazing for a young horse. That has to be over forty years ago and he hardly seems to have aged. When you walk into his yard his enthusiasm for life is immediately apparent. He'll have to show you his latest horse, strip all its rugs off, and before you ask, will have someone run it up outside. He's 90 this year! Please let me have some of his enthusiasm at that age.

I worked for John and Heather (not our daughter – his partner at the time), for a number of years and probably learnt more about horses in this job, than all the rest put together. John is a dealer, but of top-class horses. He supplied competition horses for several Olympic team members, including the Italians and Japanese, as well as the British. In the autumn he found hunters for wealthy locals. If John sold a horse cheaply, it wasn't good, and either went to another dealer or perhaps the local hunt whose expenditure was not great, but they always knew the quirk.

In the Cotswold Hunt that quirk could often be that it wouldn't jump without another horse to follow, which was something that whipper-in Roland knew only too well. Years ago, when I hunted Pat's little palomino stallion, Roland would ride over at the meet and tell me to stay with him. There were times I had to jump a fence three or four times before his mount decided he could follow. The masters of the Cotswold liked to be well mounted themselves, but were loath to part with much cash for the staff horses.

Some of the hunting clients had us in fits in the tack room. One London gentleman, whose country residence was in Gloucestershire, turned down a super horse from John because it was grey – the shade didn't suit his own grey hair. John then found him a big bay horse that acted as a safe conveyance out hunting on Saturday, provided we schooled it all week. I have no idea what the horse's proper name was, but we called him 007, licensed to kill, as he was lethal in the stable.

One slim, handsome young man, much favoured by the hunting ladies, kept two horses with us for a couple of seasons. Smiles all round when we found him applying makeup before donning his pink coat and top hat for the meet. Not quite so amusing when Scotland Yard officials arrived at the stables, checking what we knew of him.

He'd been caught in a routine security check the night of Princess Anne's attempted kidnap in the Mall. Tools of his trade had been found in the back in his Jaguar. He proved to be a well-known cat burglar.

Stewart was another of the London crowd, but totally different. A small man, John found him a lovely lightweight chestnut gelding, with a flaxen mane and tail – Blondie was 15.3hh if you stood him on high ground, but Stewart assured all his friends he had a 16 hand hunter. Stewart was a great one for classic remarks made when out hunting: asked once if he'd seen the brace (of foxes) pass by, he assured the whip he hadn't seen a pheasant all day.

Blondie was one of my favourite horses and during the summer he was one of my showjumping mounts. John would take a lorry full of dealing horses and hunters to Rockhampton, while Heather and I travelled in the Rolls with Stewart. Though it was an automatic, his driving was poor and I remember that Heather and I often arrived green and feeling sick. Between us we would jump every horse in the lorry. Some we shared, but mainly we had our own string, one of the highlights of the job. Often a young dealing horse had so much potential it was like riding a rocket and I gained some of my best competition experience.

Not that John was the kindest of teachers. When training people who'd bought expensive horses from him, his teaching methods were a little more polite. Not so with me. I remember riding a pig of a horse that wouldn't go forward. As I circled round John, trying to achieve a canter, he just watched, saying nothing for a while.

"Did you have polio as a kid?" he shouted, quite kindly, as though interested. (I was some distance away!)

"No."

"Well use your bloody legs then!" Oh, I learnt a lot from him.

Alongside the dealing and hunters, John also took horses to be broken in, having the reputation for producing some of the best in the country. We had potential competition horses from all over England who were broken to perfection, never worried or frightened. The ground-work took four weeks before anyone sat on them, by which time the horse had learnt in long reins how to steer and move forward. We had National Hunt racehorses that went on to win thousands, trainers always respecting the importance of a sound grounding.

We also had rogues. John's ability was known throughout the horse world. This meant that he was the go-to person for help when someone said, 'We've tried to break him, but it's not going well.'

On one occasion it definitely meant several people had tried to break the two new arrivals. At this point Aub and I were both working for John. Not many people know Aub can ride a horse. He's actually quite good, although it was not his preferred occupation. He and John were mainly the ones breaking colts, the name given to unbroken horses even if mares or geldings, as these two were. Heather and I dealt with the competition and dealing horses,

"Those two colts that have just come in," said Aub. "Keep well out of their way. They're definitely not unbroken, just ballsed-up horses someone's wrecked. They're frightened and they're big."

They certainly were. Strong Irish Draught types, standing over 16.2hh. One a bright bay and the other chestnut with a wide white blaze down his face. Heather and I watched from a safe distance while working our own horses as John and Aub, having fitted breaking tack on the chestnut, tried to lunge him. Even though the lunging ring was deep in mud at this time of the year, which tended to ground most horses, the chestnut ploughed through the conditions at a lethal speed, ignoring the contact of the rein on the bit in his mouth.

"Put him back in the stable and leave him in tack," Heather shouted. "He needs to learn some manners before he kills you both." The men decided perhaps she was right. We had two stone breaking boxes in the yard, each with large, heavy wooden doors that could be secured, so both horses were safe with the top door shut. Aub and John went off to do something else, so Heather and I got on with some chores. Both horses were thankfully accepting the full breaking kit of roller, breaking bit with side reins and crupper, which gave the horses something to work against. The bay was starting to mouth on the bit, saliva dribbling down his front. The chestnut was still looking ignorant, but would hopefully realise as soon as he dropped his head, he would feel more comfortable. We left them to mull over life.

It seemed like only a minute later that we glanced down the field, where some youngsters we'd turned out were cantering round. In the adjacent field, where the gate opened from the yard, were the two colts, both still wearing full breaking gear. The chestnut was also adorned with the stable door frame, which in no way inhibited him from trotting round the field at speed.

He was such a dangerous animal that for our own safety, we had to wait until the chestnut either extricated himself from the doorframe or destroyed it, the result being a combination of the two, but eventually we returned them to different stables.

Many weeks later we returned the bay to his owner. The horse was going quite well, but not a novice ride. Sadly, the chestnut was never going to be safe to ride, although I still recall memories of Aub riding him, attempting to make a difference.

Shows and jumping were both John's and my passion, and often I was coerced into acting as groom even after I'd left his employment. One of the most striking horses John had was a beautiful grey Irish Draught type, Robin Hill, known as Dobs at home. A real character; although usually the politest of horses, he could let himself down on occasions. He always expected a polo after jumping a round – once when I failed to produce one, he caught sight of a small child with an ice cream cornet, and with a lurch of his neck, consumed the ice cream in one mouthful!

I had to do a detour back to the lorry past the ice cream van to replace the stolen item, while the child's mother consoled the little boy, thankfully finding it as amusing as most of the other spectators did.

While Aub and I were both working for John we opened a new joint bank account. Having both filled in the relevant forms at the TSB in Cirencester, the girl behind the counter who was checking them, seemed a little unsure. She glanced over at Aub then back at the paperwork and said she needed to discuss something with the manager.

"Not sure what the problem is," I said to Aub. "We're not asking for an overdraft. Not yet anyway."

We waited for several minutes until she returned looking a little hassled, followed by an older man.

"I'm sorry, Mr Andrews," the manager started. "Have you filled in your occupation as a 'housebreaker'?"

"Let me have a look," I said. "Idiot!" I now addressed Aub. His writing was not that good and I could see how the confusion had occurred.

When I explained what we really did, the girl gave a look of relief, although the manager certainly didn't appear to have a sense of humour. We managed to open the account.

During the time Aub and I both worked for John, we were lucky enough to absorb many of his skills and techniques in breaking and handling young horses, something that set us in good stead when we ventured into the horse breeding and production world ourselves.

John had started his riding career in racing yards and this was where he'd learnt these skills. Sadly, John's racing career brought more falls than winners, but a chance offer by the Doney family saw the start of John's showjumping career. John was a great one for telling us stories of his past, which kept us amused on long drives to shows. He certainly had his share of success with numerous wins at major shows, but tales of his disasters, such as Kingsbridge show, were much more fun.

John arrived at the West Country show late on Friday night, to jump the next day. He and Frank, his driver and groom, had five horses on board, but needed the lorry empty to set up their beds and sleeping bags.

"Good bit of grass," John pointed out to Frank, looking

around him.

"Can't just turn them loose here, can we!" said Frank. He wandered off and returned with a plan. "I've found a tent; we could just pop them in there."

The grass was as deep inside the tent as outside. In the dark they could see little else, so the five horses were unloaded and secured in the tent for the night, while John and Frank sorted out the lorry for their night's sleep.

Birdsong woke them around five thirty and Frank wandered off to check the horses.

"Jesus Christ!" John heard him say, and ran across to the tent.

Complete devastation: trestle tables upturned and vegetables of all shapes and sizes strewn all over the grass, some with mouthfuls taken out. They caught the horses and tied them to the lorry while they took up their beds, then loaded up and left the showground, to park in a layby for several hours. Around eight o'clock they returned; amazed to hear some horses had wrecked the horticultural tent.

John also had some great schooling ideas, but not all worked out as planned. One horse, Gay Dora, wasn't keen on jumping water. On a visit to Hickstead, John made an early morning walk to test out the water jump prior to the day's competition, only to meet Pat Smythe returning from doing exactly the same.

Passing by, they smiled knowingly at each other. It was still only 5am!

When it became clear this was happening, the Master of Hickstead, Dougie Bunn, stationed a steward and caravan in the ring overnight to stop the offence. And Gay Dora still stopped at the water!

We've been great friends with John and his wife Wendy for a long time, and they proved to be a huge influence upon our plan to begin our horse breeding enterprise. They bred a lovely coloured stallion Masterpiece, out of Little Nellie, a thoroughbred Grade B showjumper Wendy had had a lot of success with.

Masterpiece was a very correct horse, with excellent movement and the loveliest temperament, which to me was so important in a stallion. Back in my journalistic days I always remember interviewing another breeder, Sam Barr at his Limbury Stud, where he produced the famous Welton horses. Sam emphasised that ability was not the most important characteristic to look for in a competition horse, but the desire to perform.

Good temperament is the closest you can get to that, and later, we would find that all the foals we bred by Masterpiece had that desire.

*Millie with one of her colt foals Work of Art,
who was sold as a breeding stallion*

CHAPTER 19

Millie and Dash

We were just recovering from the Foot and Mouth disease outbreak which devastated farming in 2001 when I was offered the chance to borrow Millie to breed a foal. Our sheep had escaped the disease itself, but 2001 was financially damaging as livestock sales were severely restricted, so I pointed out to Aub that horses weren't cloven hoofed (unlike the sheep), and this could be a useful side-project should we be affected by a similar situation again. Also, I felt the need for another horse.

I'd known Millie from a foal. Out of a bay thoroughbred mare, bred to race, by a stunning black Oldenburg stallion. Oldenburgs were bred as carriage horses in their native Germany, so they have active movement and powerful stature. In this case, the combination of bloodlines had produced a strong but beautiful filly who I admired greatly. I helped with her breaking-in and would have dearly have loved to buy her, but she was worth far more than my pocket.

Once sold, she stayed in the yard where I was working. I was able to follow her training from an uneducated juvenile to a competent potential event horse. Unfortunately, her eventing career had not gone far before she suffered a stupid accident, causing herself considerable damage. She never really returned to competition work, but did breed two lovely foals for her owner.

Millie was so easy. Lovely to handle and even Aub became attached to her; though he always assures me he doesn't need horses. The following spring she got in foal to Masterpiece and we looked forward to the possibility of a coloured foal, as quality coloured horses were now becoming the trend.

All I wanted was a healthy foal and a happy mare. Millie's first foal for us was a bay filly, Calypso, not coloured but a truly lovely model of a horse. Like her mother, easy to handle and break and she was the first we sold to go eventing. While still a foal, she was to introduce us to the very best horse we would ever have; I was concerned she needed company when being weaned. We needed another youngster.

One Friday morning in September, I glanced through the newly arrived Farmer's Guardian to see a curious advert for a Warmblood yearling for sale. Another filly, she was described as having unusual markings and I was intrigued. She was in a village in Worcestershire called Flyford Flavell.

"Wouldn't want to say that after a couple of drinks," was Aub's response, but I looked on the map and saw it was barely five miles from a farm where I was due to deliver some rams. Without conferring with the other half, I called on a friend, Hilary, who happily agreed to come with me, so arranged to look at the filly once we'd dropped off the rams.

Dash o'Paint was aptly named. A tall bay roan yearling filly with black legs, two long white stockings and a white sock, but from her left stifle it looked as though someone had thrown a pot of white paint down her hind leg. I loved her. She wasn't expensive, so I looked at her very carefully.

"What d'you think?" I asked Hilary, as I moved away from the filly.

"Can't see anything wrong with her."

I agreed on the price there and then and parted with the £100 deposit.

"You won't get her in there," the girl's husband said jokingly, as he took in the low sheep trailer I had attached to the pickup.

"If I pay for your fuel, would you deliver her?" I asked, and that was agreed.

Dash was homebred, out of Velvet, a black cob mare, who was both ride and drive, by Saiko, a bright chestnut Belgian Warmblood colt, with many white markings on his limbs and body. The girl had owned Saiko as a youngster, but since sold him on as a showjumper. Dash's papers made interesting reading. Warmbloods, the 'in' thing at the time, can be almost any breeding from Hanoverian to Westphalian, Gelderlander to Oldenburg, with a fair amount of English thoroughbred in their back breeding. Saiko went back to Lucky Boy, a top thoroughbred showjumper, whose breeding is often found in warmblood pedigrees and she certainly passed on this jumping ability.

Calypso and Dash lived happily together once Calypso was weaned, but as Dash moved into her second summer she was already almost sixteen hands high. It was decided to put her in foal, as that should slow her growth down, so she also visited Masterpiece.

In 2003 Dash gave birth to her first foal, a huge coloured colt and Heather and I were both there. It was about 4 o'clock in the afternoon. He was enormous and I felt for her, but she seemed unconcerned and loved him. We called him Scooby, although he later became Miserden Drum Major.

Scooby was a definite character. His colour markings did slightly detract from his handsome head, a skew whiff piece of brown down his face giving the impression of a roman nose from one side, but his conformation and movement were superb. He would have been about six weeks old when I first discovered his amazing jumping ability. Mother and son were in the two-acre field close to the yard, and there must have been some other horses in the field opposite the sheep shed. The two fields were divided by a double fence, each of sheep netting with two strands of barbed wire along the top, to dissuade horses from nibbling the hedge planted in between. At this time the hedge was of no height, mere saplings attempting to grow.

As I wandered into the field, hoping to take a good picture of the mare and foal, Scooby decided to show his independence. With beautiful strides he cantered towards the double fence and popped it with a bounce stride in the hedge. I was too horrified to press the shutter and have always been furious I didn't photograph his move. The youngsters in the other field approached with a speed that obviously frightened him because he turned and this time jumped the entire fence in one leap. An amazing achievement, especially undamaged, if not with the elegance of his first jump. Thankfully he didn't try to leave the field again. I'm not sure my heart could have coped.

The following spring, as a four year old, Dash went to John's to be broken-in. I'd told him I'd like to do a bit of ridden work and perhaps have another foal, as Scooby was so good. She was behaving well, but after they backed her John was on the phone.

"What you aiming to do with this horse of yours?" He can never remember any horse's names! "She might jump like a stag but she can also buck as high as the telephone wires. She's not going to be something you can just pick up and ride when you feel like it. You either take time to produce her properly, sell her, or just keep her as a brood mare." John was never anything but straight.

There was no way I was selling her. She was such a lovely horse, but on watching her in the school I realised he was right. The trouble with working full time, having a family and growing older is you lose faith in your ability. At one time I would have, and did, sit on any horse and usually got a tune out of it, but coping with Dash looked a little daunting. I didn't have the money to have her ridden on well for me, probably for the next six months seeing her bucking ability, so she became our number one brood mare. I'd only wasted £600 having her broken in!

Life never seems to come together as you'd like it to. In my late teens and early twenties, I'd have given anything for a horse like Dash to compete on. Watching her on the lunge, throw all her enthusiasm into jumping big fences, even if that enthusiasm did escape in a stream of bucks on landing. Why are talent and desire rarely matched by finance, simultaneously? Now I was able to afford a horse like her, although still on a shoestring, my best approach was to breed lovely offspring from her, probably to sell for others to ride.

Above: Scooby heading towards the fence before he cleared it in a single leap. I wish I'd caught the jump
Below: Pondering the return trip

Beautiful Dash, with one of her foals.
Photograph by Dan Tucker

CHAPTER 20

Brood Mares and Foals

Millie and Dash proved to be a useful source of income for the farm. Millie's first coloured foal, a beautifully marked colt, was sold before he was ten days old. This was down to John. He was approached by a lady wanting a coloured Masterpiece colt, and as he didn't have one to sell as a foal, asked me about ours. Aub had only agreed to have the horses if we sold some, so he was delighted, especially as the price was quite substantial.

My well handled, nicely mannered colt changed homes at six months. His delighted new owner called him Archie, but his show name was Monarch of the Glen. He didn't go on to do great things, but the trouble with breeding horses, however talented they are, their home and owner really decide on the level they'll be taken to. As long as both are happy, I could cope with the lack of future achievement of some I sold. Others went on to amaze me.

Scooby was at John's to be broken when he was sold. A lady came to the yard, looked at him over the stable door and said he was just the horse her husband had been looking for and we did a deal. He was a big foal, and we'd been worried about Dash growing very tall, but neither made much over sixteen hands.

Scooby's new owner, Ralph, was very keen to show him. He won in hand then Ralph decided to show under saddle – not in working hunter classes as I thought he might, as Scooby's jumping ability simply went from strength to strength, but as a show cob. It didn't take long for Scooby's love of food to help change his body shape and Ralph had a great season showing him in the ring. This was one combination which had high hopes for the future.

The following season Ralph put Scooby at livery in a top-class showing yard. I never thought the new rider did the horse as much justice as Ralph, but he was a name, essential for success in the showing world. A world as close to nepotism as they come.

At one time the sheep showing world was similar, but thank goodness the old school fashion for putting up a friend's animal above a superior one has mainly gone. Show judging is based on one person's opinion, on the day, and none of us are perfect. I've judged classes myself and in retrospect felt I should have placed animals differently. But at that time, on that day, my choice was right. As an exhibitor, I've stood in the line next to an animal showing so many faults I would have hung it up as a meat lamb, only for the judge place it in his top three. This can be repeated when judge and competitor meet at a later show and their roles are reversed. It happens.

It's probably the reason why, with horses, I competed mainly in the jumping arena, where a pole knocked down cannot be argued about.

Ralph kept in touch, assuring me that Scooby would make it to the Horse of the Year Show. I was dubious, cobs should only measure 15.1 hh and I was pretty sure he exceeded that when I sold him. Then came the real crunch. Ralph had asked the producer if they could go to a HOYS qualifier fairly local to him, but was told the ticket for that show had already gone! This meant he knew who was going to be judged as the winner before the actual show day. He also went on to assure Ralph that they'd win at a named later show. So Miserden Drum Major was the first we had bred to make it to the Horse of the Year Show.

Obviously I went to watch him. Ralph secured me a pass and as I stood up to the horse in the collecting ring, he was definitely nearer sixteen hands than fifteen. He didn't come in the prizes so nobody had reason to object and it was a wonderful occasion to see one of our first foals in such prestigious surroundings. It just left a bitter taste that the route to get there revealed to me some of the uglier sides of showing.

The following season, Ralph took Scooby home and competed him himself in maxi-cob classes, where height wasn't an issue. They had a great season.

Our next mare Amy and her foal were bought over the phone, one cold February Sunday morning. A friend had ended up looking after this mare and foal when the owner had a few medical problems, and thought I might be interested. Always one for a deal, I tried to be a bit practical. Having been told this was an ex-racehorse, with foal, I asked her age. She was eighteen. No, I wasn't interested.

"What about the foal?" She went on to say she was a bay filly. As we were now attempting to breed coloureds I lacked enthusiasm.

"Look, they've been left here, totally neglected. Her field is freezing cold, I'm chucking the odd bale of hay out to her, but she needs the foal off her." There was a short silence.

"Is it straight? No problems?"

"It's a nice foal."

"Okay. Not more than £500 though."

Within the hour the poor, half starved mare arrived in the yard with her foal, whom she'd done well. Obviously we had now taken on a job lot. I would have liked to put a warm rug on the mare, but the foal was going to live with her for a while as I felt weaning would be too stressful. So we simply put them in a warm, well bedded barn with ample hay and water. I don't think I saw Amy without hay in her mouth for the first week.

The filly was sweet. Happy to be handled and a good sort. The paperwork arrived, showing Amy had raced just a couple of times, not too successfully, before being bred from. The foal was by National Hunt stallion Midnight Legend, who stood at a stud fee of £1000!

After a little homework into Amy's breeding I discovered this was her second foal by Midnight Legend. The first had been bought by a Scottish trainer. When Racer, as we called the foal, was three I contacted the trainer, who was thrilled to find a sibling of the older horse. He had several successful wins under his belt and after negotiation Racer left for a racing career in Scotland. 'Sea the Stars' was the horse of the day, so Racer was christened 'See the Legend'.

We had great enjoyment following her career and placing successful bets.

Miserden Imprezza, known as Pretzel at home, was one of the most talented we bred. Some years ago, John gave me her mother, a near thoroughbred mare, Impedimentia, (Impy). Sired by TB Impecunious, by Derby winner St Paddy, she was out of a very successful four-star event mare, Flying Finnistere. Due to an accident as a two year old, Impy hadn't competed, but had already produced Tina Cooke's top eventer, Faeresferre, and several showjumpers for John. When put to their coloured stallion Masterpiece, she still threw bay foals, which was his reason for passing her to me. As luck would have it, her first foal with us by Masterpiece was a coloured filly.

Impy left us several good youngsters, all by Masterpiece. Having sold some as foals, I'd decided we'd keep Pretzel, and produce her as a competition horse.

Aub and I started her ourselves, having had plenty of experience doing this. Working well on the lunge, I knew my talents for long-reining were not up to John and Wendy's, but at that time they were working with polo ponies and had shut the yard to breakers.

With heavy heart I contacted another local yard, who assured me they had the expertise to continue her education. I'd explained she needed at least two weeks in long reins, so was surprised and annoyed to see her ridden the following week, but assured she was hacking out well. Watching Pretzel work in the school, lack of long reining immediately showed she'd never learnt to go forward. She napped, dropped her shoulder and bucked her jockey off. This wasn't a one off. She'd obviously mastered this trick.

She came home immediately and was turned away until John and Wendy were able to take her, but instead of one of my usual straightforward youngsters, they found her a very damaged horse. Taking her back to square one, they slowly improved her attitude. After a six week stay, three weeks of which were dedicated to driving in long reins, evasion was still apparent. At John's suggestion she went to a friend of theirs, Stuart, a tall, experienced horseman who re-backed and rode her on.

Pretzel showed great talent loose schooled over fences, but I needed a jockey who could ride her. Only about 15.3 hands high, this needed to be someone smaller than Stuart, and again on John's recommendation, I approached Bex, a local show jumper.

When Bex took Pretzel on she knew her history, but luckily fell in love with the mare. Although Bex was occasionally bucked off, the mare's show jumping talent was obvious, and Aub and I enjoyed watching her jumping, and winning at County level. After a successful summer, having sold her own two competition horses, Bex announced she was going to Australia for the winter; sensible girl. She obviously felt the same as me about British winters.

Pretzel had qualified for the Blue Chip Winter Championships at Hartpury the following March, and we felt she was going well enough for another good rider to take her on. Advertised as 'Quirky, but talented show jumper' with a price that justified this description, we had several replies. Two riders tried her, and while I felt the first was the better jockey, the second wanted to buy her. Sold with the full knowledge that she could buck for England, the woman was very keen to have her. Bex and I were both horrified when she was collected in a single horse trailer, but Pretzel was persuaded in and off she went.

Apparently, her journey was a nightmare, her new owner having to drive up the hard shoulder when the motorway was blocked, as Pretzel panicked in the confined trailer when stationary. Over the next couple of months it became clear the new owner was struggling with Pretzel, but I had neither the finance nor the jockey to buy her back. Accepting I'd sold the horse in good faith, but the pair hadn't bonded, she decided to get some professional help. Things went from bad to worse.

All credit to her owner, she rang me later in the year, offering Pretzel to Bex as a gift, as long as she collected her in a horsebox the following day. Or she would be shot. She had thrown a very experienced horseman and was far too dangerous for her to ride.

Bex brought her home, climbed on and within a few weeks was winning again. Pretzel had now learnt to nap out hacking on her own, and suffered from claustrophobia when travelling, so needed extra space in the lorry, but Bex coped with both problems. Horse and jockey had a rapport that survived. Bex took Pretzel through to Grade A, topping the Southwest Silver League points Championship for numerous weeks. Sadly, she failed to qualify for the Horse of the Year show, tipping a rail in the jump off of the qualifier, after winning 118 previous classes with no poles down. Last year, Pretzel became the proud mother of a Vangelis-S colt. We hope he will achieve the same as his mother and more.

CHAPTER 21

Births and Caesareans

The problem with choosing to make my life's work revolve around breeding animals is that sometimes I feel as if it all hangs on a very fine balance, with happiness and tragedy only separated by one quick decision. It's harder because I care.

A few years ago, the second week of March was madness, even though we had lambed a considerable number of ewes during February. I even had to represent Aub at his Aunt's funeral; he was unable to leave the sheep shed with at least one ewe lambing every half hour. Luckily, Aub's aunt had been a sheep farmer so we knew she'd understand the situation.

However, a few days later when all seemed to have settled down a bit, it was my turn to be left in charge while Aub drove up to Stoneleigh for a Texel Society meeting.

Having by now resigned his position on the Board of Directors, he was still very involved with Breed Development, and this was a meeting he couldn't really miss, although I cursed the Society for having meetings at this time of the year.

"Don't worry, if you have a problem give Mark a shout," and off he drove.

Mark T was a local man who helped us out one day a week, and Aub's advice was all well and good, but I knew that on Wednesdays Mark worked somewhere where he was unlikely to have phone signal. Fingers crossed.

All went well during the morning, but by lunchtime I was aware of a first time lamber, scanned for a single, looking very uncomfortable. She was a ewe we had thought would lamb with the February bunch, but must have missed her first breeding cycle and taken the tup again. His raddle was faint so we hadn't seen a mark. This didn't bode well as she had probably been fed towards an early lambing and had by now eaten far more concentrate than we would normally feed a ewe having a single.

Around two o'clock she started to show she was lambing, but I decided to ignore her for another hour. A young ewe needs time to open up, so I was not rushing in. Eventually I had to catch her, easier said than done, and investigate as things were not progressing as I would have liked. She had a huge lamb, thankfully coming correctly, but well and truly stuck.

After a lot of lubrication and massage I wasn't getting very far. This birth was going to need more strength than I had, as well as luck to get this lamb alive. The ewe had opened up well and I'd been able to secure the wire behind the lamb's ears and, after a struggle, attach ropes to both front legs. Once the tension on the lambing rope drops, as you sort the other out, the lamb pulls its foot back and you find you've lost the first; but now I had both secured. Nothing was giving. I was aware that it was still going to be a tight squeeze getting this lamb out. People often say a woman is better than a man at lambing because she has smaller hands. While to an extent this is true, often a larger hand and arm are necessary to open the birth canal wide enough for a big lamb to come out. This was one of those occasions. The ewe's contractions were weakening.

"Hold on darling. I'm doing my best." I knew she was too.

Stop, recalculate. Need more strength. I phoned Mark T. No reply. I may not get this lamb alive, but I would try. I rang the vets and explained the situation.

"I need muscle, not one of the girls". The receptionist laughed and promised she would have someone with me as soon as possible, but I was aware the vets were a good twenty-five minutes away, even if one was available immediately.

I cursed Aub and his meetings. I'd started to cry; frustration making me despair. Snap out of it. You're a farmer. More lubricant. Ropes and wire rhythmically pulled then relaxed. More lube. Something must move. I seemed to have been struggling for hours, and it probably was at least half an hour.

"Please don't get up" I begged the ewe. By now I had her wedged at the front wall of the sheep shed, so I could get purchase pushing against her, sitting with both feet against her backside. Nothing like Call the Midwife! Again, I pulled as she gave a final effort and gradually, out came the longest lamb I'd seen for long time. Exhausted, I untangled the ropes and wire and the lamb lifted its head and baaed. The ewe, too tired to stand, greeted her child who I lifted round and put in front of her, having rubbed its nose with straw and cleared its airways. She licked it, talking softly in response to its bleats.

I sat in the straw, exhausted, watching the miraculous

scene before me. I didn't think I'd get him alive. A few minutes later a car drove into the yard and Paul, our strong burly vet got out.

"They said you needed muscle," he smiled.

"Go away," I grinned stupidly. "I've done it!"

"So I see. Good result. All OK?"

I told him I thought so and he left. It was so rewarding to find that this little ewe loved her lamb so much after all the struggle and discomfort she'd been through. I left them bonding, while I made a well earned cup of tea.

Sadly, not all situations turn out this well. I can't remember waking up during any lambing, however bad the weather, feeling as depressed as I did one morning last year. We'd lost three lambs the previous night, and although two were situations we've come to realise you have to accept, the third should have been in a pen with his mother this morning.

The dramas all seem to happen in the evenings, when our daytime lambing staff have gone home for a hot shower and early night. In the early evening a Charollais cross had given birth to twins; the first coming backwards, something we seemed to have had more of than in previous years. This lamb was difficult to get, but quite viable to lamb with her being a Charollais cross, the lambs are always a little more pliable than the pure Texels. A good pure Texel is just a bundle of powerful muscle, built like a British Bulldog, and if too big or with a difficult presentation may need intervention, but the crossbreds don't usually give us that problem.

Aub successfully lambed the first one, and while it was

wheezy, having taken in fluids, we soon had it breathing, although not with any great enthusiasm. Straw was stuck up its nostrils and I put my finger in its mouth to encourage breathing that way, and eventually it seemed to catch on to the process. At this point I usually explain to them that it can become habit forming if they just try a little harder!

The second lamb came correctly, but refused point blank to breath. Again, straw up the nose and massaging, but nothing was going to revive it. By this time the first had decided that breathing was too much like hard work, so a disastrous lambing and a very sore and sad ewe. Hopefully in the morning we would take two lambs off the feeder and she'd happily adopt them.

We were well into the evening when another ewe lambing obviously had a problem. This was one of our smartest Texel ewes whom we'd come to know so well during the long hot summer. Nicked by the shearer, a tiny wound had opened up to a large sore on her back once the summer flies had attacked. She was treated numerous times, becoming easier to handle each time. Animals soon become aware when you are trying to help them. We applied antibiotic spray and latterly Stockholm tar to keep the flies at bay and eventually brought her into the sheep shed, where she and a friend lived for several weeks, as this was the only place we could maintain the healing process. Outside, even through the Stockholm tar, the flies were continually opening up the wound. Eventually we won the battle, but she was easy to recognise as the top of her quarters were still stained black from the tar. We caught her easily and

Aub tipped her up, lying her down making investigation easier.

"What on earth have you got here girl? Feels like a breach. All I can feel is the hocks."

I held her tight as Aub struggled to push the lamb further back inside the ewe, enabling him to very carefully turn the legs from their crouched position to the feet coming first, the only way to consider lambing her.

"God, it's got enormous feet, might need a caesarean. Hang on though, I'll try." He continued to feel along the legs. Making the decision he pushed the feet back inside.. "This won't come out alive like this. It's too big to come this way. You silly girl, why couldn't you have one coming the right way?"

By now it was the emergency number I was calling. I told them the problem and we needed a caesarean. They assured me a vet would be in touch. When he rang I told him we needed to operate, the lamb was huge and coming backwards. He said he'd be out. We prepared the operating site. I topped up lambs requiring a feed, held difficult ewes still while their lambs suckled, then topped up the milk bucket. All the bottle lambs were now successfully grasping that warm milk was on tap and life wasn't so bad.

"Any chance you could ring Mark to give us a hand?" I said to Aubrey. Our son would be happy to help, I felt sure. "An extra pair of hands would be useful?"

By now it was half past ten and I was exhausted. The thought of another hour in the sheep shed with a caesarean was almost too much, but it would have to be done. "Shall I go home and turn the supper off now, or wait until we have the ewe on the table and we're waiting for the local to work?"

"I've rung Mark, he's coming to help," said Aub. "You can go when he gets here."

Music to my ears. I was just so tired. Doing the night shift is okay if you don't have an active part in the day shift.

The vet arrived and we brought the ewe round from the shed to operate in the grain store, where we'd set up a useful table. Aub explained that he'd moved the lamb from hock first position but it's just too big to come backwards. As Aub held the ewe we both thought the vet was simply examining her and would come to the same conclusion. Before we had time to blink he had pulled hard on the two feet and back legs just showing and was pulling the lamb as hard as he could. By the time Aub, still holding the ewe, realised what he was doing, it was too late. The vet had pulled the lamb too far to change his plan, but of course it wouldn't come. Using all his strength he eventually got the back half of its body out, but it was well and truly stuck on the shoulders, as we had anticipated it would be.

The best way to describe a lamb's shape is triangular. It is similar to an arrowhead going into something. Going the right way this is reasonably straightforward, as the shape of the head, shoulders and rib cage follow on from each other. In reverse, like the shafts of an arrow, the rib cage is wider at the back and very difficult to extricate.

It seemed a long space of time before the lamb was eventually removed from the ewe. I could have cried. We already knew this lamb had been killed, by the vet doing exactly what we didn't want to do. He started massaging the lamb and feeling for a heartbeat. "No heartbeat. It's dead."

Aub gently lead the ewe to a lambing pen, gave her a bucket of water then walked off to the far side of the yard in disgust, only returning to give her antibiotics and a pain killer. The vet, hopefully realising what a profound mistake he had made, kept trying to revive the lamb to no avail.

"Next time when we ask for a caesarean, please do a caesarean. Aub could have pulled the lamb out if he'd thought he'd get it alive," I said, as civilly as I could. Hindsight is a great thing, and we should have stopped him pulling the lamb quicker, but it all seemed to happen in a flash. Why do we have a certain faith in professionals?

The morning's depression turned to tears at lunchtime when I discovered our lovely, friendly ewe dead in her pen. Not only had the vet killed her lamb he had obviously damaged her irreparably.

Chapter 22

A & E

Summer brings the excitement of shearing. Seeing what last year's promising lambs look like, without their winter wool, usually happens in May. June sees the main ewe flock losing their wool, when it's often so hot they're extremely relieved. Shearing is definitely a welfare issue. If we didn't do it, the sheep would have fly eggs laid on them, and hatching maggots can eat a sheep alive. Now it often costs more to have them sheared than we receive for the wool, although not many years ago the wool cheque could pay the rent or the winter feed.

When we were still grazing any available land offered, we rented some fields at Caudle Green, next door to another farmer, Julian, and assisted each other whenever necessary. On a bright sunny morning, I was setting up the yard and small barn, anticipating the arrival of Lawrence, our shearer, when Julian popped round. He kept a small flock of pedigree Rouge de l'Ouest Sheep in some adjacent fields, and asked me if I had time to hold some of his lambs while he tattooed them. This wouldn't have been too testing a job when the lambs were small, but because he had to wait until he had help, Julian had allowed these to grow quite big – so holding a fairly strong lamb was somewhat more difficult.

At that time, we also tattooed Texels for identification purposes. Now, I'm pleased to say, we just use tags. Tattooing in the ear is a skill. You have to place it between the numerous veins on the ear to limit bleeding. Julian was not the most skilful that morning, probably not helped by me struggling to hold the animals still. On a number of occasions Julian missed his aim and a vein was nicked and by the time we finished I was covered in blood. Ears are prolific bleeders.

Lawrence, our shearer, raised an eyebrow at me when he arrived, but carried on setting his machines up as normal. We worked well together, him catching and shearing while I rolled the fleeces, all going fine until later that day he somehow managed to glance the shearing blade against his calf muscle. A true professional, he finished shearing the ewe.

"Hang on Lawrence, let me deal with it properly," I said, running for the first aid kit. I had antiseptic wash and a dressing, but typical farmer, Lawrence was already dealing with his injury under the hosepipe. It was quite a gash and I suggested A & E. Being sensible, he realised the cut was bad enough for stitches, so I applied my dressing and we drove to Cheltenham.

Parking at this hospital is usually impossible, but for once I found a space quite easily and led Lawrence inside. The receptionist glanced up, horrified as I explained the situation, Lawrence's wound still bleeding profusely through my makeshift dressing. A nurse rapidly appeared and directed us to a smaller waiting area and it wasn't long before Lawrence was taken into an examination room. As I flipped through the magazines lying around a couple of people looked into our secluded waiting area and quickly backed out. Before long Lawrence reappeared, leg dressed in swathes of bandage, a prescription for painkillers and instructions to rest the leg.

"That's the quickest I've ever got through A & E," I said, walking back to the car.

"Have you looked at yourself?" Lawrence laughed. I glanced at my bloodstained shirt, the result of the morning's tattooing. "Between us we look like something from the 'Chainsaw Massacre' and probably stink to high heaven of sheep. They were just glad to get us out of the waiting area."

After a good laugh Lawrence assured me he'd finish shearing the last few sheep before he drove himself home. We're a tough bunch, us farmers.

On another occasion it was a pony that forced me to visit A & E. I'd bought him to ride, and possibly sell on at a profit, but had found him difficult to clip, although he was sold to me clipped out. This was another occasion when Mary was on hand, as she was still helping me with the last of the lambers. She expressed great concern and offered me dire warnings about not getting hurt. I assured her I was taking precautions, having dressed the pony's neck and chest in an old jute rug, fitted as a bib, offering me protection if he tried to rear up.

Obviously, it was not sufficient protection, as he did rear up and caught my right temple with his shod foot. I sat down in the straw, my hand covering my face, resting my head against the stable wall.

"You idiot," said Mary. "You've got a hoof print on your face. Come on, I'll drive you down to A & E."

I protested for a moment, but she insisted.

The weather was still cold and we were dressed in our usual lambing uniform of tattered Barbour jackets and terrible old waterproof trousers and wellies. I think we checked our bottoms before we sat down in the empty waiting room, but in general unless you fell backwards this was the last area to be covered in filth. The same could not be said for our fronts, we were plastered in lamb scour, stale milk, iodine spray, silage and mud. Our inner clothes may have been cleanish, but our outer garments did for the whole lambing season. It was a pity we'd not taken time to think about changing into something a little less revolting, but Stroud A & E had said to get there quickly while they still had their X-ray department up and running as it was now early evening.

Despite the pain and shock, I began to doze off. We were still at a stage in lambing where, if not vertical, we were comatose within a few minutes. The next thing I was aware of was the appearance of a doctor.

"Bloody Hell," he said, aghast. "What's that God-awful smell in here?"

Mary and I looked at each other.

"I think it's us" she said.

"Let's get you in and out then, as quickly as possible."

Back at home, our daughter Heather, now living in Edgeworth, had called in on her way home from work to discover her father in a very irate mood.

"Your mother's been kicked in the head by a horse and

there doesn't appear to be anything organised for supper."

She then had the full story from him, including the information that I was in no great danger and the X-rays had shown no serious injury.

She laughed. "Look Dad, what's the real emergency here? Mum at the hospital or you haven't had your supper?"

"Mum's alright. She's got Mary with her. I've no idea what to have for supper!"

In fairness to him, he'd also been working 24 hrs a day in the sheep shed, but we did laugh about this afterwards.

I still bear the scar above my right eyebrow.

CHAPTER 23

Holidays

Days off are rare but when they do happen, farmer's aren't the best people to take on holiday. They really prefer to stay at home and work. If persuaded to travel, they're constantly looking over hedges to check whether other's crops or lambs are as good as theirs, which can make you feel as if you're still at home.

Aub's childhood holidays were mainly spent visiting relatives on their farms, where he was in his element. My childhood holidays were good, and probably equally energetic, but considering how much sheep were later to become a big part of my life thanks to Aub, for me my encounters with them on holiday were often negative.

My father's great love was the Lake District. From the age of nine I was burdened with a rucksack and hiking boots, ready for a week or ten days of walking the fells from one Youth Hostel to the next. Both prolific photographers, my parents were in their element as the ever-evolving landscape rolled out before us. The weather was not always kind, but I soon learnt atmospheric conditions make good pictures. There was also the endless wait for the sun to emerge from a cloud to produce an artistic masterpiece. Inevitably, while perched on a small mountain, I'd become aware that just a few feet away was the carcase of a dead sheep, lying on its back with its legs in the air, having been trapped in a gully. Any suggestion that we moved was treated as an irritation, although Mum did start to back me up after several similar macabre encounters of her own.

She was also a godsend when we spent a night at the Black Sail Youth Hostel, set deep in the fells, miles from any form of civilisation. Or so it seemed.

The youth hostel was an old shepherd's bothy converted into two dormitories, one each for male and female hikers, each housing four bunk beds. It was idyllic. We loved to sit outside on the wooden bench and gaze along the valley, disturbed only by a few curious sheep. But these sheep and lambs were another source of my distrust of the species. They threw themselves against the dormitory door during the night, violently, like vampire sheep trying to break in. Thankfully, my mother explained this noise. They were just settling down to sleep against the warm wall.

The nearest road was over two miles away, accessed by a mountain track which was no problem to the warden, who brought in all the hostel supplies on his motorbike and sidecar. A wonderful cook, he produced sustaining breakfasts and suppers, after which we washed up in bowls of warm water on a table outside. Water drawn from the nearby stream was piped into the kitchen and I remember one walker asking for water from the kitchen rather than washing and cleaning his teeth in the stream. Little did he know the water was exactly the same, although I think they checked for dead sheep upstream!

Probably my closest encounter with a sheep, at that time, was when one of the hikers caught a lamb for me to stroke. We christened him Wonky as he held his head on one side, but he appeared to be quite happy with life and thoroughly enjoyed the fuss, having realised walkers were good for the odd sandwich.

Not all the fell sheep had good manners. Many years later we introduced our children to Youth Hostels, and were heading for the summit of Helvellyn when the mist clamped down. I was about to sit on a stone cairn when it turned into a Swaledale ewe who actually attacked us – possibly for not producing the required sandwich. Not one of our best days. Heather, about eleven, was in floods of tears because she really didn't want to walk to the top of Helvellyn. I was in the dog house, because after taking one photo of Aub and the children at the summit I ran out of film. Cloud was descending fast and the last views of Striding Edge were not inviting, but being seen off the summit by this irate sheep was the final straw.

When the children were in their early teens we ventured to camp sites in France. This was much better. Heather and Mark had a great time, but Aub was usually so tired to begin with, all he wanted to do was sleep. Once the children had explored everything near our camp site on foot, Aub was still snoring in a deck chair, so I suggested I drove them somewhere. Amazing how quickly someone can regain consciousness at the thought of their wife driving the car on the wrong side of the road. From then on, we spent more time visiting places than staying on the camp site.

Sheep still featured though. We took the train to Paris, visited Versailles and looked at French Merino sheep at Rambouillet, where they lived in the splendour of a purpose-built farm, similar to a castle. I drank a lot of red wine and we all enjoyed the cheese. On one site, with a golf course, we saw huge toads on the fairway. One morning I discovered one under our bed. Perfectly harmless, but not an ideal bedroom companion. I refused to get up until Mark removed it.

Now that our children are grown and have families of their own, if we go anywhere these days, other than a sheep sale or show, Aub is happiest pointing northwards. Travelling south down the M5 is his worst nightmare – and when I suggested a holiday in Cornwall, he certainly wasn't over-excited.

"Why there?" he grumbled. "It's miles away, jam-packed with tourists" – he obviously didn't include us in that description – "the weather's crap and I hate seagulls!"

This wasn't worth answering. Having been brought up on the South coast I love the sound of seagulls. Aub always laughs when I say seaside gulls sound different from the farmland gulls, but they do. I can immediately smell salt in the air, and hear the sound of waves softly lapping against a stony beach. Oh yes, I was looking forward to everything relating to our seaside holiday.

We'd been invited to join our son Mark, daughter-in-law Kate, two grandchildren and Kate's parents, to stay in a lovely house on the south Cornish coast for a week in early May and I was looking forward to it. We'd done the same the previous year, but not stayed the full week due to other commitments. A whole week was obviously daunting to my husband. When we arranged with Mark T, Aub said, "Not sure when we'll be back."

"Next Saturday," I said.

"Hmmm, I'll let you know," he grunted.

At that point I made sure there was enough room for me in one of the other cars. He could travel back alone if that was his plan.

It wasn't long before we had our usual argument about the sat-nav.

"What do you mean, you can't remember the postcode?" said Aub.

"We don't need it yet. Straight down the M5, through three counties, before we're anywhere near it," I said. The sat-nav annoys him almost as much as I do – it would be madness to turn it on now.

"You'll have to ring Mark and get the postcode."

"Okay, but not yet."

The M5 was busy, as usual. The sky was grey and the forecast promised worse weather further west. Not the most exciting prospect for a beach holiday with our grandsons, but after six weeks of lambing, followed by the inevitable aftermath of sick sheep and bottle feeding, a break of any sort sounded wonderful to me. And once Mr Grumpy got into holiday flow, I knew he'd appreciate it too.

We stopped at the motorway services to pick up coffee and parked away from the major throng to eat our picnic. I knew the hard-boiled eggs would go down well, but half expected comments on excessive salad in the rolls. I pointed out it was healthy, which fell on deaf ears.

"Ring Mark and get the postcode of this house," he said as we left the services.

"Okay, but you won't be able to put it in until we stop next."

"Doesn't matter, just get it. Then we know where we're going!"

I did as I was told, only to be greeted by a surprised Mark on hearing where we were, having expected us to be closer. They'd arrived. We stopped just after Exeter to put the dreaded postcode into the sat-nav.

"I do know where we're going and I can read a map," I said. The last part of that sentence was met with a wry smile.

"I trust this stupid sat-nav woman rather than you. Is the Tamar Bridge a toll bridge? She's asking if we want to avoid the toll."

I checked on the map. "Looks like it, but that's the way we need to go."

We continued on the A38 for some distance until suddenly told to take a left turn.

"Why?" I ask. "We need to stay on the A38 for Saltash."

"Well what do I do? She says turn left."

"Perhaps she knows a short cut. Or you've pressed something you shouldn't have, like saying we don't want to pay a toll."

On the other hand, if I insisted we stay on the A38 and the traffic was bad it would be my fault again. "You do what you want."

We followed the sat-nav round smaller roads, shopping centres and eventually came the instruction to turn left for the ferry.

"What ferry? Aub exclaimed. "We don't want to go on a ferry!"

"Well, go straight on back to the A38" I suggested.

We crossed the Tamar Bridge and travelled the south coastal route, until the sat-nav tried to send us up to the A30 – the more central route. And that was when Aub realised we still had almost two hours to go before we 'reached our destination'.

"Why have we come this way? We're miles out of our way. We should be on the A30."

"Last year you said how unattractive the scenery was on the A30," I said. "I thought we'd try the prettier, southern side of Dartmoor, it's no further. Let's turn the bloody sat-nav off, we know where we're going and we'll recognise it when we get there."

"No."

The weather gradually worsened, the skies darkened and the wipers were on full bore. A tuneless rendition of 'Here comes Summer' emanated from the driver, whose mood was as foul as the weather. As we approached Porthleven we spotted the lake where Toby had hoped to go boating last year, but it had been closed.

Further on I pointed out the left-hand turn, and to my amazement the stupid sat-nav woman agreed with me. Within five minutes we'd arrived. Thank goodness, a massive hug from each grandson, a drink at the adjacent pub, supper and a good

night's sleep, would improve the holiday mood.
Even better, there wasn't a sheep in sight.

The famous photo from the top of Helvellyn,
the only one I took before the film ran out

A real holiday at last –
feet up and not a sheep in sight

Thelwell through and through:
Mark on Ella (left) and Heather on Charm

Chapter 24

Pony Club Camp

With our rural situation and the wonderful riding opportunities in Miserden Park, both children became fairly competent riders by a very young age. With that in mind, Pony Club activities were an obvious choice during the school holidays and these culminated with a week at Pony Club camp each summer, which Heather and Mark both enjoyed. Sadly, when I asked them about their highlights, neither could remember much of their equestrian achievements – except that both immediately said 'the bun run'.

This was the arrival around 10.30 every morning of orange squash and a delicious range of bakery sticky buns. They could even remember their favourites.

Camp usually managed to coincide with the start of harvest, so Aub was fairly happy having sandwiches for lunch for the week as I often helped out with the lower rides at Junior camp.

Their first camps were on the Shetlands, Ella and Charm, when they were both in the same ride, and infighting could be a problem. However, my memories of one of the later Pony Club camps stands out above the others.

I shut the ramp with both ponies safely loaded in the trailer on the Sunday afternoon.

"Right, have you got everything?" I asked.

"We only need ponies, don't we?"

"Probably helpful if you have a saddle and bridle."

"Mark could always ride bareback," Heather grinned. Mark had spent most of his time riding Ella, his Shetland pony, around without a saddle.

We drove towards Northleach, then down the lanes to junior camp and unloaded Pebble and Squirrel. Both had had their back shoes removed, like the other ponies in the field, this being the safest way to keep them all together for the week. As ours were geldings they were in the same paddock, the mares were separate to avoid arguments. They whinnied to other ponies when turned out, but soon settled down to the important business of finding something to eat. The paddocks were never too flush with grass to keep the ponies from gaining weight over the week. It was easier to add a hay net or small feed if necessary, rather than have a gorged pony full of grass trying to be athletic.

Once the ponies were established, we drove into the yard to sort out security for the tack. Heather and Mark found one or two friends doing the same, but eventually I dragged them away. They'd all meet in the morning.

The following morning we arrived in plenty of time for first inspection at nine o'clock. All seemed the usual chaos I remembered, with the odd loose pony trotting round looking for its mates while a small child ran after it waving a head collar.

"Hang on, Ed," I shouted. "We'll corner him in the barn."

I soon had pony and jockey paired up and pony safely tied up in his allocated section of the barn. Heather collected their head collars and before long everyone had their ponies saddled and ready to leave for the field.

"Right," shouted Julie, their instructor. "Blue ride, Ben in front, then all in single file to ride up the lane to the field. Sue, as you're my assistant, can you follow at the back to check we still have everyone when we arrive?"

Glad not to be in sole charge of the string of eight-year olds, I finally shut the field gate behind them so all the rides were secured. Heather had joined some of her friends in another ride, looking both competent and happy.

A large level field had been allocated for all five Junior rides to share, with some areas roped off for jumping arenas. Julie Weston, a little older than me, was kind, sensible and capable of keeping a group this age under control without spoiling their fun. As usual, the first day was spent sorting out the rides. All children should have attended a rally the previous week to assess their capabilities, but at least two in Julie's ride had failed to turn up and I felt one of those, Marcus, should be in a lower ride, though the move wouldn't be popular. I mentioned this at lunch and Julie and I agreed to see if he managed any better during the afternoon.

"He'll hate being put down into the green ride, they're all much younger. If he could stop knitting with his reins and keep his weight in his heels, he'd be more secure and have

163

better control over the pony. I'll find a shorter pair of reins or just tie a knot in them so he has more contact with Ginger's mouth."

A bigger concern was that the portable loos hadn't arrived. Where there should have been eight portaloos, the entire camp of fifty-three children and at least a dozen adults had to share one toilet in the farm workshop. Small boys were being directed into the bushes.

"I've rung the office," the district commissioner assured everyone. "The worrying thing is they left Ledbury at six o'clock this morning and should have been here by half past seven. Nobody's seen them."

Most of the children found this hilarious.

"Not quite sure how the girls at senior camp would have reacted," Julie said to me, grinning.

"If they're older versions of Heather, I've a pretty good idea."

The afternoon was devoted to fun and games, as the morning had been more than testing on the little ones. Marcus blended in better and knotted reins did help. He was quite an athletic child and luckily his pony seemed to have resigned himself to the start of a week at camp.

"S'afternoon was better than this morning," grumped Mark on our way home after they'd help turn their ponies into the paddock, had tea and cleaned their tack, something they both hated. "I'm tired," he yawned.

"I thought we'd just pop to the harvest fields and see Dad with some tea when we get in. Are you too tired for that? At least you can amaze him by telling him you cleaned most of your bridle."

Mark brightened up at the thought of a ride on the combine and Heather agreed.

Tuesday morning and still no loos. Everyone was getting slightly disgruntled at this point. The DC had rung again only to receive the same reply as the previous day.

"Don't be ridiculous. If they left you yesterday morning surely someone must know where they are. Can't you contact the truck driver?" She was not a lady to be fobbed off with silly excuses. Headmistress of a local private school, described by a pupil's mother as 'a galleon in full sail', she swept through camp keeping everything in strict order. Later that morning a message came through saying our loos had gone elsewhere, but hopefully others should be with us by lunch time.

Sitting at the instructor's table enjoying an excellent lunch, I could hear Mark and his friend, Ben, muttering as they ate their sandwiches. Afterwards, I wandered over.

"Round the bollards, round the bollards, that's all Miss Weston kept saying all morning," they complained.

"You all need to sort your steering out," I said. "Once you learn to manoeuvre round the bollards, she'll stop nagging you, so it's up to you to shorten your reins and control your ponies. I'll suggest some bending races this afternoon, then you'll have to steer them properly if you want to win. There might even be prizes."

At the mention of prizes, the boys cheered up considerably and Julie threw me an appreciative glance. I had a bag of sweets in my car for such emergencies. As I wandered out to collect them, Steve, one of the fathers helping out, drove off up the road.

"Where's Steve gone off to in a hurry?" I asked, back in the barn.

"To look for the portaloo lorry," said Julie. "Not sure if sending our first aid man away is such a good idea, but our DC is beginning to lose the plot with the loos. Have you seen the queue in the yard for the farm toilet?"

"Yes, I was just about to join it. I'll find a bush or we'll never get the ride back out again."

Bending races, first at a walk then a sedate trot, seemed to fit the bill for both steering and competitive small boys, although as always there were a few complaints about people cheating, mainly from the two girls in the ride.

"Can't we just finish off the afternoon with a walk, trot and canter race?" Lucy asked. She usually won her favourite gymkhana game – her pony walked very fast, then trotted faster than most of the others could canter.

"I don't want you all racing each other at speed so we'll start with just a walking race and then maybe a walk and trot to finish with," said Julie.

Everyone seemed happy with this especially Lucy who won the walking race with ease as the other ponies were either too slow or broke into a shuffling trot. This meant they had to turn a circle, or in most cases, where the jockeys still had limited steerage and circling was not an option, were disqualified.

"Could we just do a slow walk and trot, Miss Weston, please Miss Weston?" requested most of the children.

We agreed that should be safe enough.

"Right, turn your ponies round, away from the gate, and walk up to Mrs Andrews, no trotting or you'll be eliminated, then you can trot the last bit back to me. I want to see you riding nicely at a rising trot, not coming as fast as you can, and there'll be an extra prize for style," Julie added, having checked there were enough sweets left.

Off they set at a sensible walk pace, even Lucy not kicking her pony on. They'd almost reached me when Ginger turned his head pulling the reins out of Marcus' hands. He'd seen another ride heading towards the gate to go back to the barns. Spinning round he headed after them at a spanking trot with Marcus looking like a member of the flying trapeze as the vigorous motion sent him airborne. The other seven ponies took a split second to register that one of their party was leaving and suddenly it was like the charge of the light brigade. I did my best to catch Pebble's bridle as he went past, but Mark was the least of my worries. He was quite a competent rider and used to galloping off out hunting, but several other ponies ejected their jockeys. The scene was carnage.

Leaving others to catch the ponies at the closed gate where the leaving ride were watching in amazement, Julie and I rushed to check that no child had been badly damaged and were pleased to see them climbing to their feet, if a little tearful.

"Absolutely typical for it to happen when the first aid man is out looking for loos!" I muttered to Julie as I dusted a crying child off and assured myself that she was frightened rather than injured.

"Wow, that was great," shouted Mark, having shortened

his reins up on Pebble and trotted back to me. "All Marcus's fault, but great fun, can we do it again tomorrow?"

"No, you damn well can't" said Julie under her breath, grinning at me.

Having reinstalled all jockeys on their ponies, some now being led by additional helpers from other rides, a loud cheer erupted from the ride in front. The loo lorry had appeared on the road.

"That's a relief, in more ways than one," I said. "We didn't appear to need first aid, but probably better just get Steve to have a look at the casualties."

To our relief the rest of the week fared well. The weather was wonderful, if a little hot for the afternoon rides and several juniors were invited to swim at the lovely outdoor pool in the private grounds. Mark thought this was highly preferable to a baking hot ride.

On Thursday, when Mark and the rest of the blue ride went swimming, I watched Heather doing a very nice dressage test on Squirrel. All boded well for display day on Saturday and hopefully a place in the mini eventing team; Squirrel could jump almost anything.

At lunch time on Friday, Julie and I sat together to discuss prize allocation for our ride after the following day's display.

"We've got eight rosettes. I think Lucy can be 'most helpful' even if she is a bit of a know-it-all. I've seen her kindly showing one or two of the others how to clean their tack properly."

I agreed and actually suggested that Marcus should be the Most Improved Rider.

"His escapade flying off on Tuesday has meant he's sat far

more deeply and concentrated on keeping his weight in his stirrups and at last he's sorted his reins out."

"Best at cleaning tack?" Julie asked.

"Not sure, but don't think Mark will qualify for that!"

All parents were present to watch their children's displays on Saturday morning. Julie and I had organised a sort of handy pony competition, involving both bending, to show how much their steering had improved and ending with a course of tiny jumps that also needed accurate steerage to complete. We were both quite impressed by the progress in our ride over the week and grateful we'd got this far without serious in-fighting or injury.

Awards were given out to all rides; Mark was delighted to have won the afternoon's competition and be awarded the 'most competitive' rider. A few murmurs could be heard from the audience who thought the taking part was far more important, but as I pointed out to Mark – who would want to just take part at Badminton when they could actually win? This made his day. Some of the bigger rides were unable to award prizes to every member, but as one father explained to his child, he'd been 'mentioned in dispatches.'

Heather and Squirrel did a great dressage test and very neatly completed the small, but slightly complex show jumping course, gaining her not only a rosette, but inclusion in the mini eventing team for the competition the following week. They continued competing in numerous Pony Club teams throughout the summer, having great success.

The final straw in Heather's eventing career came at a schooling session in a local indoor arena. Children and ponies were cantering down a line of fences, when, sadly, Squirrel made up too much ground through a combination. He turned at the end of the school far quicker than Heather anticipated, and I still have visions of my poor daughter hitting the far wall and sliding down it, rather like a cartoon character taking a cut-out of the wall. Unfortunately, I wasn't aware of how badly she'd damaged herself, although I didn't make her get straight back on and did take her to the doctors. But her competitive riding career then ceased until she read Jilly Cooper's *Polo*. A new episode of her life began.

Bigger ponies and more speed

Chapter 25

Polo

Jilly Cooper has a lot to answer for. Heather read *Riders* and thoroughly enjoyed it. By this time she had tried most aspects of equestrianism without great success or enjoyment. Not long after reading Jilly's *Polo* and loving it, the Pony Club suggested their members took up the sport. Heather needed no encouragement. Polo was to be her next calling.

"You know you said you and Dad put some money by for Mark's and my further education," she started tentatively. "Can we talk?"

I was putting the finishing touches to supper. "Mmm ... take the potatoes into the other room, please. Can we do it over supper?"

Coming back into the kitchen she was frowning, "S'pose so. Really wanted to talk to you first."

I looked at her questioningly. "If you want to discuss your further education, I'm sure your father would be interested too."

Heather had struggled with some academic subjects at

school, particularly maths. Even her teacher had asked if she really needed GCSE maths. Things went further downhill at sixth-form college. Her social life was great, which it would be, spending more time in the Slug and Lettuce in Cirencester than at lectures. When the A level results came out poor Heather was devastated, while we were not surprised, it simply illustrated her lack of work. Sadly, it was difficult for us parents to gauge how much or little effort she was putting into her subjects. Heather was bright and didn't really have to work too hard to achieve good grades. But obviously she should have done more.

Heather was fifteen when she started thinking her further education might move away from the academic. It was probably a good choice and her decision not to go to university was a relief to us all. Her request for a polo pony came as a surprise.

"Why?" said Aub and I simultaneously.

"I'd like to do Pony Club polo properly, but Squirrel isn't keen on a mallet, and all the others in my ride are doing it. Fenella and Diana have now got polo ponies and Sophie's pony's happy to play, but Squirrel's frightened and takes off if I swing my stick. Mum, there's a really nice pony for sale at JonP's. She's too slow for Fergus, he's selling her and she'd be great for me. She's a real Argentine polo pony, bit like a quarter horse. Can we see her?"

This all came out in one excited mouthful. Aub and I had already discussed Heather's future. Admittedly polo hadn't crossed our minds, but maybe allowing her to have her share of the savings wasn't so silly.

"OK. What's she like?"

"Dark bay; originally came over from Argentina and she's played with Fergus, but his grandfather also hunted her. You've seen Mrs F riding her round the village."

I had seen our neighbour, Sally – Mrs F to the children – riding a very nice cobby sort round Miserden and thought how lovely she was. We went to look.

I remembered the mare well. Apparently, she knew the game inside out, but as Heather had said, wasn't fast enough for the more professional game her owners were now playing. She stood just over fifteen hands, was thirteen years old and more expensive than half our savings. I think she was the most expensive horse or pony I'd bought so far, but on vetting it came as a pleasant surprise when the vet thought she was probably only eleven.

Porty was the loveliest horse we ever had. Heather adored her and I was quite happy exercising her as well. Although safe, she certainly wasn't a plod. A long striding walk and bouncy, balanced canter made her a gem to ride. So, polo was the next venture.

Polo is hockey on horseback. You hit a ball into a goal with a stick. With two teams of four players on each side, each game is divided into short, often fast, six minutes sessions known as Chukkas.

Heather was working for a couple of young polo players, Paddy and Jason at weekends and holidays. In professional polo each player has four or six ponies, depending on the level of the game. Each is played for the six-minute chukka, then changed for the next one with a very short interval between chukkas. The pony lines are usually some distance from the ground, under trees for shade. Grooms tack up the next pony, hop on and ride it to the polo ground to exchange for the played pony. Often players need the tack taken off pony one for pony three while playing on pony two, then pony one must be washed down and made comfortable. All this happens within the six minutes. When working for Paddy, Heather remembers Jason helping her to tack up and telling her to speed up.

One day at Cirencester Park, Paddy took her down his line of ponies and told her the order he wanted to ride them in, where his spare sticks were, etc. He pointed out all were fine to ride down to the ground, except Rabbit. She should just lead her down for the changeover.

"Whatever you do, don't ride her."

Of course, in the panic and heat of the moment, having ridden the others, Heather forgot his warning. She jumped on Rabbit to her immediate regret. Rabbit hopped and bucked all the way round the pony lines and up and down alongside the ground. All she could hear was the thunder of hooves as Paddy galloped up behind her shouting, "I told you not to ride her."

Still, all ended well, according to Heather, if a little challenging!

Her lessons from the boys continued once she started playing properly, with Paddy and Jason cheering her on from the side when they could. Some of the girls couldn't believe how lucky she was to know Jason; he was a heartthrob and now played for Black Bears.

She was still having the occasional lesson with Paddy,

though she often complained he spent more time chatting up girls who rode past, rather than concentrating on teaching. Once, trying to impress one of them, he smacked a ball straight into Heather's back, an injury she was aware of for several days.

I suggested, to gain more experience, she applied to work for JonP at the weekends. JonP owned and ran a private Polo Club, about a mile along the road. She could cycle there. Not too enthusiastic about this, Heather was enjoying the college and polo social life. Nevertheless, I hauled her out of bed at weekends and sent her to Edgeworth. Once, suffering from the worst hangover possible, after throwing up down the side of one of the horses then turning two out in the paddocks still wearing their boots, she was sent home in disgrace.

By this time, Heather and Porty were an established partnership and playing regularly. The great thing with Pony Club polo is you don't need a full string of ponies, like the professionals. The chukkas are held throughout the day, with at least three-hour intervals, so each player just rides one pony. The competitive season runs through July and mid August, with additional matches throughout the summer, culminating with the Championships at the prestigious Cowdray Park Polo Club, West Sussex.

Heather joined Sophie, Diana and Fenella and they formed the Cotswold 2nd Team, playing in Loriner and Rendall (the names given to the sections for their age groups). Porty was a well-built type, never going to be the fastest against the little thoroughbred ponies, but brilliant for riding the opposition off.

In one match played high up by the airfield on Aston Down, Heather rode her opposite partner right off the pitch and into the pony lines, with a skill only to be admired. Both he and his mother, from a well know polo playing family, were furious, his mother accusing Heather of taking his stirrup off.

"Lucky she didn't undo his belt," said Jenny, a friend, watching from the sidelines, bent double laughing. It was at this game that Lisa, one of the organisers offered Diana and Heather the opportunity of six months in New Zealand, playing polo. Sophie was a year too young to go, but Heather and Diana jumped at the chance.

It's distressing to say, and hopefully does not happen now, but we found some of the coaches favoured certain families; usually the affluent, who hunted. Basically, we did everything on a shoestring, but we still did it. Sadly, Heather and Mark had both been made to feel they weren't 'quite up to standard'. Their ponies were 'adequate', but not top class or expensive, often being on loan. So far, we'd succeeded well with the polo, but the crunch came when the trainer at the time obviously had someone wanting a place in the team. He took Heather to one side and told her Porty was too fat and unfit and she was out of the team. Had this been true, I would have agreed, but Porty was a different build from most of the ponies. I was furious. Both Heather and I had taken weeks riding her up and down our Cotswold hills, ensuring she was in peak fitness.

To qualify for the Championships at Cowdray, the teams had to compete at several competitions and the loss of this chance would put Heather out of the running. She was devastated. Luckily we were contacted by the manager of The Wilton Pony Club who were a player short for the qualifying match game at Tidworth. They welcomed Heather with open arms, now having a team to compete. Sophie and Diana were gutted that Heather wasn't playing with them. No more so than in the third chukka of the day where the Wilton played against the Cotswold, and beat them!

Luckily the powers that be soon sorted the situation and Heather was back playing for the Cotswold the following week at Windsor. She still had great loyalty to her new found friends from the Wilton and was delighted when they also qualified for Cowdray.

Our car was now a reasonably respectable Subaru, capable of towing the double horse trailer I'd managed to borrow. In preparation for the championships it was piled high with everything we needed. Porty was loaded in the trailer, along with most things other than the kitchen sink. We were camping at Cowdray so cooking utensils, food and bedding along with the makings of a homemade tent cover for the car were essential. I thought the car had everything we needed, but it wasn't until well past Newbury, that I realised I hadn't been hit on the head by a carelessly placed polo mallet.

"Have you got your sticks?" I asked.

Horrified, Heather undid her seat belt and rifled around in the back, but it was fairly obvious these vital pieces of equipment were still in the front porch.

"Can we find a phone box?" – we didn't have mobiles in those days – "Dad can take them to Sophie's, they're not coming down till later today."

It doesn't usually happen this way, but just ahead loomed a lay-by with a red telephone box. Thinking I'd be more coherent than our agitated daughter, I rang Aub.

"I'm not bringing the bloody things down to Cowdray, we're just about to go combining. Why didn't she check she had everything?"

No sympathy there, but after explaining all he needed to do was take them to Daglingworth, he became more co-operative.

We prayed he'd catch Sophie's family before they left. I was sure we'd be able to borrow a stick, But Heather insisted she needed her own. "They fit me. I can't borrow someone else's."

"Anything else we've forgotten?"

"Don't think so." Heather glanced round the crammed car. "I just thought I'd leave them till last, then forgot."

"Don't worry. Dad might moan, but he'll get it sorted. I'll just check Porty's okay."

Thankfully, the rest of our journey was fairly uneventful. We unloaded Porty and settled her in her stable. Our parking spot appeared to be opposite the local golf club. Other parents were booked into hotels in Cowdray, having towed caravans down for their children to sleep in, but as usual, camping suited us. Not that I had much sleep – the golf club partied until late each night.

The main polo ground at Cowdray was impressive, with the ruin of an old castle in the background. The parade of teams from the six year olds in Jorrocks through to the adults in Gannon made a tremendous spectacle. A mass of colourful shirts and different coloured ponies, it heralded the start of a wonderful weekend.

It was hot and lack of rain in previous weeks meant the ground was like concrete. Each group had four teams, who all played each other during the first day through the three chukkas, spread from 9am to 5pm. The semi-finals were the following day.

On the Saturday evening I was worried about Porty, who'd found the hard ground testing. She was almost leaning against the stable wall, trying to ease her discomfort. One of the older girls offered me two sachets of Bute.

"Is that okay?" I said, concerned about any rulings on drugs.

"You'd take a couple of aspirin if you felt like her, wouldn't you," she said.

Later that evening, Porty had perked up considerably. If we broke any rules, I wasn't going to worry.

The Girls' Cotswold 2nd Team had been very competitive to reach the Championships, but even Sue, the team manager warned them that the likelihood of beating one of the other teams was remote. However, in the middle play-off the following day, should they beat this team, it would put them in with a chance of third place rather than fourth. Play was quite slow and the man with the loudspeaker growing less enthusiastic by the moment, trying to give a commentary on a game with little happening. Both teams were too well matched. Eventually there appeared to be a sort of stalemate in front of the Cotswold goal. None of the players seemed able to get to the ball to drive it into goal, but after several minutes the commentator shouted with excitement.

"Give that pony a sugar lump. Goal to the Cotswold."

Dear old Porty, possibly fed up with the lack of action, had actually kicked the ball between the goal posts herself.

Exciting, but draining, after that weekend at Cowdray I knew there was no way I could drive back to Gloucestershire that night. As luck would have it, we had some very good Texel sheep breeder friends close by who did B & B. David and Maureen were wonderful. They gave Heather and me a beautiful room and Porty a field to graze for the night as their guests. The chance of a warm shower and a good night's sleep was heaven. They were life savers; I will never forget their kind gesture. I couldn't remember ever being so tired and we slept well into mid-morning.

The homeward trip should have been uneventful, but the memory still sends shivers down my spine. We found ourselves behind a convoy of army vehicles, all going just that little bit too slow. Whether I forgot I was towing a trailer I don't know, but I decided to overtake on the duel carriageway. Sailing along, the road suddenly started to slope away from me and I realised I was going too fast. I had my happy, chattering daughter alongside me and the best horse in the world in the trailer, and I was an idiot. With the trailer I couldn't brake to any great degree, I gradually slowed the car down through the gears, managing to pull into the left-hand lane, no doubt stopping at the first opportunity.

Thank goodness Heather was unaware of the risk I'd taken, but next to falling asleep driving the truck and trailer back from the Royal Welsh Show, this rated as one of the most heart-stopping moments of my life.

Heather and Porty (left) on the Cotswold 2nd Team

A photograph of Mark (right) riding and leading
polo ponies in Cirencester Park from the book
A Century of Polo by Herbert Spencer

Chapter 26

Mark's Riding career

Mark's riding career took a vaguely similar route to Heather's. An annoying little nine-year-old who needed to be occupied, I suggested he might like to take Pebble hunting when hounds met locally at Henley Farm. Of course he didn't want to, so Pebble stayed out in his field, covered in dry mud, the result of excessive rolling when the field had been wet. Now all was bone dry, it was going to take a bit of effort to clean his grey coat, so part of me was relieved I only had one pony to clean for the day's hunting. That was until about quarter past ten on the day of the meet, when Mark, finding himself with nothing exciting to do, decided to go hunting after all.

Heather's pony of the time looked fairly immaculate for a cream coloured hairy in the middle of winter and Heather, as always, was dressed correctly in jodhpurs and tweed jacket. Not so Mark.

"I'm not wearing jodhpurs," he insisted. "They're horrible. I'll wear my jeans and green coat." So, mounted on an extremely muddy grey pony, with his jeans tucked into long socks to stop his legs getting sore and a bright green anorak, with Heather pretending she didn't know him, we made our way across the field to the meet.

The day was one of misfortunes. A big bay horse kicked out at the meet, its metal shod hoof just making contact with Mark's thigh, luckily at the end of his kick. Although obviously painful, any closer it would probably have broken his leg. One of the worries of small children on small ponies out hunting.

When hounds moved off, Heather joined some friends trotting along the tarmac drive while Mark and Pebble, or probably Pebble, insisted on going straight along the rutted grass, gathering speed to catch up with those of longer legs, ahead of him. In doing this he changed from trot into canter, then very rhythmically took tiny jumps over the slightly higher bits of solid mud in the rutted landscape. Mark had not been expecting this, and after about three of these little jumps parted company with Pebble, ending up sitting on the ground, upset and cross.

I reached him to see tears running down his cold, red cheeks, and on seeing me his expression turned to anger. It was all my fault. I'd made him go hunting and Pebble had kept bucking until he fell off. Gathering him up, checking he was ok, I couldn't help smiling at his description of Pebble's actions, which did little to allay his bad temper. Once Pebble was caught, he agreed to ride him home, as the alterative was to walk, but said I could sell the pony as he never wanted to ride again.

Mark's riding career ceased for a number of years. Pebble was lent to some friends who then bought him and kept him for life and Heather continued with a variety of riding activities on her ponies. Heading into his teenage years, Mark decided he needed a holiday job to finance his preferred lifestyle.

"Well, there's two options, I guess," I said, having pointed out I had no intention of running him in and out of Cirencester each day. "Looks like it's either the Carps" – Miserden pub, The Carpenter's Arms – "or JonP's, he's always needing staff, especially by this time of the year. If the pub's got nothing, give him a ring. You can bike to either."

This went down like a lead balloon, but eventually the grumpy young man, (takes after his father in attitude), rose from the horizontal position on the settee and cycled off.

I knew JonP at the local Polo Club would have fallen out with and sacked half his staff by the end of July, when school broke up for the holidays. He was so grumpy to work for, his staff often found somewhere else by this time in the season, so I was sure he'd be happy to pay Mark to help out. What I hadn't expected to hear were JonP's compliments on his riding ability or to see a picture of Mark happily riding one horse, leading two others down the main ride of Cirencester Park. This photo is in the book *A Century of Polo* by Herbert Spencer.

Mark was to surprise me again, on one of his returns from university, when he said he fancied a ride on one of my young horses. Tawny was a sixteen hand thoroughbred mare and I had to say Mark looked well on her. Although only a baby, I'd no worries about her temperament or behaviour, so one morning Mark and I rode Tawney and Porty around Miserden Park. It was really nice, just the two of us catching up with his new life at uni in such a happy relaxed way. That was until I realised that the local Territorial Army division were practicing manoeuvres in the park. Not too much of a problem until we heard a helicopter hovering overhead and realised it was aiming to come down in a nearby clearing.

We were riding through the woods, probably out of sight. I could feel Porty, who was so used to all situations, now tensing under me. Glancing at Mark, who was still chatting nineteen to the dozen, reins in one hand, cigarette in the other, I realised his laid-back approach was just what young Tawny needed and the whole event passed the two of them without problems.

In fairness the helicopter wasn't close enough for us to feel the downdraft, but almost! Another thing Mark has inherited from his father is his laid back, casual attitude to riding.

Chapter 27

The Enduro

This is a poem I did write, feeling rather inspired after the event!

> *Three men rode the Enduro one wet summers day*
> *One did it legally – two didn't pay*
> *The weather was bad, it hardly stopped raining,*
> *As they clung to their bikes wishing they'd done*
> *   some training.*
>
> *Thought they'd photograph well, so we stood by the gate,*
> *Cameras poised for the action, and then the long wait.*
> *The rain came on down, but we waited there still*
> *And eventually sighted them over the hill.*
>
> *One poor chap who was riding a three-wheeler bike*
> *Got caught in a rut and tripped over his trike.*
> *A hand waved in anguish was all we could see*
> *As his bike pinned him down from the neck to the knee.*

They slithered down Slad, the conditions got worse,
Down the bank they flew off with many a curse.
On through the wood, they were tattered and torn
"Who's that idiot riding straight through the corn?"

As the day progressed the weather improved
By now Aub and Joe to the patio removed
To partake of refreshments. Hot tea and pills
While Vern bravely struggled his way up the hills.

They continued to ride to the end of the day
Enjoying it all – or that's what they say,
But the following days saw the aches and the pain
And the promise that they won't do that again!

As horses have been the love of my life, so motocross – scrambling with a motorbike – has always been Aub's. It's how we met, in fact.

Trouble was, it's really a young man's sport, and by the time he'd reached his mid-thirties, Aub was returning from practices on his uncle's farm in the valley aching from head to toe, saying he'd sell the bike before it killed him. That was why an Enduro appealed to him.

An Enduro is a sort of old man's replacement for scrambling, though it was never described as such within Aub's earshot. A timed trial, not a race, with all competitors starting off together and after a set time the one who's completed the greatest distance is the winner. Actually, on the day, I'm not sure how many of the rules were adhered to.

Joe, one of Aubrey's many cousins, was involved in an event on his father's farm at Harcombe. It had rained all night. Aub had slept soundly, always exhausted at the end of a hard week on the farm, but I'd been aware of the unseasonal heavy rain and gusts of wind overnight. When I opened the curtains it was a fairly depressing sight outside for a summer's day, but Aub had already leapt out of bed with an air of unconcealed excitement.

"Wow, should be good today. The ride down Slad'll be awesome. C'mon, let's get going."

"Be a bit hairy as wet as this, won't it," I said, searching through an untidy pile of clothes on my side of the bed for a clean pair of socks.

"Na, it'll be good. Sort the men from the boys."

Speeding downstairs to let the ducks out and give the dog a quick run, he called back a fancy for bacon and eggs. Cooking breakfast, I smiled, just wondering who might be sorted out today.

"We won't have to pay," Joe had said earlier. "We're family and we're hosting it. Should be good. Vernon's coming. He's paid his entry fee, of course."

Vernon was Maggie's (Joe's sister) husband. Straight in all respects, he'd be horrified if Joe suggested he consider himself exempt and go free.

Although Aub had known about the event for several months, his and Joe's training sessions appeared to have been short bursts of enthusiasm on odd Saturday afternoons followed by throwing themselves onto the grass and consuming many cans of cold beer.

By nine o'clock, well fed and watered for the morning's entertainment, we set off for the event, Aub's bike securely loaded on the bike trailer he'd made some years ago, but had few outings these days. There was to be a barbeque at lunch time, so other refreshments weren't needed.

The farm was a hive of activity when we arrived. All the sections were due to start at ten o'clock and most of the competitors had unloaded and were making their way down the track to the valley and the start. Joe was waiting in the yard, fiddling with something technical on his bike. He glanced up at the lightening sky.

"Shouldn't rush if I was you, might dry up in a bit. My sisters are here – Maggie and Sal are going to watch from the six-acre gate, if you want to find them, Sue."

The earlier promise of skies clearing came to nothing and steady drizzle continued. The roar of bikes leaving the start line attracted their attention, persuading them out onto the veranda to watch as the leaders came into view in the distance.

"S'pose we'd better get ready and join in," said Aub.

They went to unload his bike and retrieve Joe's from the barn. I watched them put an awful lot of exertion into starting their machines and eventually riding off into the valley. Then, clad in full waterproofs and armed with an umbrella I wandered off to find the girls. The roar of bikes was immense as they passed close by and the variety of machines and riders interesting.

"Sue! Where've you been?" Sal shouted and waved. "We've

been waiting here ages to see them go by, we're soaked. Vernon's been past twice, no sign of Joe and Aub."

"They've only just gone down to the start. How's Vernon doing?"

"Safe and slow," said Maggie. "At least he'll return in one piece, I hope. The track's lethal. Who'd have thought they'd end up with this weather when it's been so nice up till yesterday?"

"Not fair is it? Gosh, what on earth's that?"

I looked in amazement at a young man riding a three-wheeled machine, in a sort of 'sit up and beg' position. I'd never seen one before, it didn't look very safe.

"I think he's already been on the floor, still he's quite game sticking with it. Here they come; they've caught up with Vernon."

We continued to watch as the rain came on down, but on the following circuit were amazed to see Joe was covered in mud.

As Aub had anticipated, the steep bank down Slad had caused its problems. When he and Joe arrived there, they met a wall of worried bikers too timid to ride down. Not to be daunted Aub rode past them down the hill at speed. Joe followed, but skidded on the wet ground, parting company with his bike. Then to add insult to injury both he and his bike were run over, the damage to his front brake making his ride around the rest of the course interesting.

We stood at the gate for what seemed like another hour and though bikes were travelling past at regular intervals there was no sign of our three again. We could see quite a lot of action in the distance. It looked as though the chap on the three-wheeler was upside down. Then we caught sight of Aub on a totally different track from the other riders. Some furious comments came through the loudspeakers about the person riding through the corn being banned next year. The roar of bikes continued through the rain, then the loudspeakers crackled and went silent.

"Let's go back to the house," Sally suggested. "They must have broken down."

Wonderful barbecue smells attracted us towards the barn where, of course, we found the men. Bikes in a heap and Aub Joe and Vernon collapsed in deck chairs looking as though the few laps they'd completed had finished them off.

"Training beneficial then, boys?" I asked.

"Oh, we're getting too old for this," Aub stretched back in his deckchair. "Anyway, the officials are getting a bit above themselves."

"What you mean, when you rode up the tramlines through the barley?" said Vernon.

"I was in the tramline. I wasn't damaging the crop. That bloke falling off his trike caused a pileup. I couldn't get through any other way. Are the burgers ready yet?"

Scrambling was definitely a thing of the past, but I wasn't so sure that these three would cope with many more enduros either.

Covered in mud but happy: Aubrey (left)
and his cousin Joe

Mr Tumness

CHAPTER 28

A Fallow Deer called Tumness

It was a Wednesday evening in August 1985. Aub returned home at half past six, an unusually early hour during harvest.

"I think I've got another deer for you to rear," he said, washing his hands.

I was horrified. This was the last thing I wanted to hear. Three weeks ago one of the lorry drivers carting corn had brought me a fallow deer fawn who'd been caught on the front of a combine. For some reason the fallow deer were producing young much later than usual, possibly due to weather conditions. I'd rushed her to the vets, but she'd only survived for 36 hrs. In retrospect, perhaps we shouldn't even have tried to save an injured wild animal – the ordeal of anaesthetics, drugs and travelling, after the shock of her injuries probably proved too much. I was heartbroken. The last thing I wanted was another fawn.

Aub had been combining the oilseed rape. For most of the morning he was aware of a fallow doe diving in and out of the crop, just after lunch he saw her again and stopped. There, still wet, lay a small new-born fawn, struggling to stand. Knowing not to touch the fawn as the mother may abandon it, he left the patch of rape and combined the rest of the field.

"I've not seen the doe come back to it. Don't know what to do. The chap's coming to chop the straw later this evening. I'll either have to move it to the side of the field or bring it home or he'll chop it." We agreed if he could see any sign of the doe when he went back, he'd move the fawn on sacking. I wasn't really surprised when it came home.

While Aub unloaded some fresh straw, I picked up the beautiful little animal from the floor of the pickup and carried him into the shed. Staring at me with big brown eyes, he was too weak to object, his long slim neck falling against my shoulder.

Teaching a fawn to bottle-feed is not the easiest of tasks as their mouths are very narrow, and restraining him was difficult. His neck and legs were so delicate and willowy. Eventually, by half drenching him and half working his mouth in a sucking motion, as we teach lambs to suck, I managed to give him some milk.

We barricaded the shed doorway with two bales of straw and tied a mesh dog guard over the top, allowing plenty of air to circulate while the bottom section was draft-proof. He soon established his sleeping area in a corner provided by a wall and the bale I sat on to feed him. At first we had an infra-red light on at nights, later I just banked the straw up around his sleeping area. To begin with I cared for him alone. When I went in the shed, he would lie still, just staring at me. I talked to him quietly, stroked and pushed at him as I thought his mother might, to make him get up. We contacted a deer farmer who suggested feeding Lactol, an expensive milk feed made for puppies, with a much higher fat content than lamb's milk. Obviously the right choice as he rapidly put on condition.

While assuring the rest of the family he mustn't become a pet, he still needed a name. Bambi had been the obvious choice for the first fawn. We named this one Mr Tumness after the little half man, half deer creature in The Lion, the Witch and the Wardrobe. I was later to receive a few phone calls from people who'd rung earlier, only to be told by the children that I was in the shed with Mr Tumness.

Tumness was most handsome. His body a soft cinnamon colour with white dapples and a black stripe down his back to his tail, the underside of which was a snowy white warning flag. The soft, mouse brown velvet which covered his head fell into wrinkles around his eyes and ears. After his bottle he would skip round the shed for three or four minutes while I watched his curious antics. Obviously, my presence gave him a sense of security because as soon as I turned to leave, he would prepare to lie down.

For the first five days I fed him four hourly, day and night. It's one thing to feed a baby in the same or next room, quite another to get dressed and wander down the garden at 3 o'clock in the morning. The only advantage being no nappy to change. One night, I recall dashing to the shed through a deafening thunder storm and feeding him with torrential rain beating down on the tin roof like gunfire. Amazingly, he was quite unperturbed.

As Tumness gained confidence, Heather and Mark were

able to talk to him and stroke him. Mark took to sitting on the bales with his feet dangling down. Wary of this new body at first, Tumness soon gained confidence and sniffed his boots. Even at five Mark had great empathy with animals. In a very quiet voice, he said "Tumbluss will soon know me. He already knows my wellies." And he was right. Later, in the garden, Mark would rush at the fawn, who would feign fear then immediately return for another game. Heather and Tumness were a little more timid of each other, but both soon gained similar confidence and she remained interested in him long after Mark grew bored and searched for fresh dragons to slay.

At six days old we decided Tumness had been confined long enough and must discover the purpose of his long legs. In a wild state he would have followed his mother through the woods much earlier. Once the barricades were down, he bravely followed me a short way into the garden, where, confronted by an array of children's swings and climbing frame his courage vanished and he shot back to the security of his shed.

Five minutes of quiet coaxing achieved the desired result. Aub and the children were stationed at intervals along the roadside wall. Although he was small, fear could make him attempt to leap this. Fortunately he was far too intent on simply galloping. He tore up and down the garden, squeaking with delight, stopping at regular intervals to investigate something, then running back to tell me all about it. I don't know who enjoyed his exercise most, him or us, but at the end of ten minutes he was the more exhausted.

Now, destined to survive, we had to decide on his future.

All along I knew we couldn't keep a wild animal as a pet. Besides, our three foot stone walls would not contain him for long. So, with the rest of the family visualising a magnificent fallow buck with a huge set of antlers standing on a snow-covered lawn during the winter, I began to ring round.

The local RSPCA recommended their Wildlife Sanctuary at Evercreech, near Taunton, who agreed to take him. They assured me their aim was to return rescued wildlife to its natural habitat, but if Tumness was too tame, as I felt he was, his future would be secure in a deer park.

The last morning he was with us, Heather gave him his bottle. We were all sad to watch him skip and run around our garden for the final time. Cousin Judy and I transported him in the back of her car, happily curled up in straw in a safe travelling box.

Until weaning in a few months time, his new home was to be a large pen with natural undergrowth and shelter, surrounded by a twelve-foot-high wire mesh fence. He was popular with visitors, the topic of a local newspaper article and, to the children's great excitement, appeared on an early morning television programme. After weaning alongside a roe deer fawn, he was released in a private deer park in North Wales, where he settled in well.

I feel our lives were infinitely richer for having known Mr Tumness.

Aubrey at Three Counties show, 2012.
Photograph by Catherine MacGregor

CHAPTER 29

Autumn and Lanark

There is nothing more beautiful than a crisp autumn morning on our Cotswold farm. Not cold, simply chill. The view across the valley is of swirling mists, layers of light gauze folding quietly over each other. Trees explode into colour overnight. The occasional flash of red flames into autumnal glory, a mix of fire and honey. Cultivated fields are laid out in dark chocolate, beige stubble with patches of pale green regrowth. A distinct aroma of pine – amazing how good fallen foliage can smell.

A shepherd's year begins in autumn, which in itself can be a moveable feast. While we don't always need new rams each season, we may still buy one. Carrying out the inspections at all the National Texel sales, Aub will often spot a good lamb. Hard not to buy, especially in years when prices seem far lower than they should.

The National Texel sales run in the autumn – from the end of August to the beginning of September, starting with the major Scottish sale in Lanark, working through to the Welsh, the English at Worcester and finally Northern Ireland. For many years I've limited myself to Worcester, where we usually sell, and have bought some very good ram lambs in the past. Rarely highly priced and sometimes smaller lambs, which suit us better as they haven't been pushed too hard and over-fed. Most purchases have been very successful in our flock.

Two years ago I decided to see what all the hype was about at Lanark, where the most expensive Texel lambs are sold. Some produce top class progeny which are seen in the show and sale rings the following year; others whose progeny are rarely heard of!

"You're only looking," I was told. Aub did admit that it was only the very striking or the problematic lambs he had time to notice while inspecting, so I could pick out any that caught my eye. I marked the details of about twelve.

I'd never been to Lanark before and was amazed at the size and strength of many of the sheep. Most with the compulsory beautiful head and huge black tear drops, but I was looking for length and backend as well as a pretty face. It was interesting to watch others select lambs from pens and run them down the walk way to see how correct, or otherwise, they were on their legs.

"What you found then?" Aub couldn't resist asking, once he'd finished the inspection. He took my catalogue and smiled, "Mmm. Probably can't afford any of them, but let's have a look."

We spent the next hour wandering around the pens, at some stops selecting my lamb and seeing how he walked. We were both quite pleased with my choices, which soon looked even pricier when several became winners in the afternoon's show. The following day's auction showed I wasn't the only one with good taste.

Nothing was purchased at Lanark or Worcester that year. Aub had already bought a ram lamb he liked at the Royal Welsh Show. Not a winner, but placed lower down the line and looked a good sort when seen outside. We also had two good rams, bought as lambs the previous year, so we were well set up for Texels.

I'd liked a Blue ram lamb at the Royal Welsh, but he'd already changed hands for a large sum of money. However, later on I was very pleased to purchase his full brother, who we named Giles, after his breeder. Then came an email from our friends in Northern Ireland, was I interested in two good ram lambs?

I shouldn't have, but Janet's photographs persuaded me to buy Colyn, too. She delivered him to the Carlisle sale, where he attracted quite bit of interest and I managed to secure him a trip home.

All farmers enjoy their way of life, we wouldn't swap with anyone. But I think pedigree sheep farmers are the luckiest. Rams will breed the year of their birth, and though we don't breed from ewe lambs (letting them mature to yearlings), some do, so the genetics of the breed can improve every year.

Using a new ram, and even one we've used lightly as lamb the previous year, brings excitement and extra enjoyment to lambing. I've lost count of the times Aub has looked at a new born lamb in the early hours and said, "That's going to win at the Royal" or "That'll make some money." Usually a fatal remark – if the chosen animal lives up to expectations, it dies just before it reaches the sale ring. But that anticipation is what drives us all to produce a top-class winning animal.

The ewes are synchronized to come into season simultaneously, and our rams work hard to do their job over a short period. The main lambing period is condensed to a week to ten days when we employ lambing staff. Then, usually a more mature ram is left with the ewes to catch any that have failed to get in lamb. Sometimes the rams are left in too long and a third cycle leaves us with another set of lambs, but this year we decided to be sensible. The rams stayed out with the pedigree ewes for the return cycle, then were brought back in for three weeks until rams were put out with the forty commercial ewes, and a final backup put out with the pedigrees. This gave us a three-week break. Hopefully, the commercials would lamb in glorious April sunshine, along with any later marked pedigrees.

The main National Sheep Association ram sales on the Royal Welsh showground at Builth Wells are a sight to behold. Thousands of rams change hands in a single day with numerous auction rings running alongside each other in all the buildings, with washable surfaces, implemented since foot and mouth. Still a great spectacle, but nothing could compete with the marquees full of rams, each with its own auction ring, when the sale was held on grass.

Other improvements include the use of ram taxis: quad bikes with trailers and drivers, available at a small charge to deliver purchased rams to the buyer's trailer. A great idea, especially when you have bought from several rings. This efficiency contrasts nicely with many farmers' original means of transporting their rams home. Smaller animals can still be seen leaving the ground in the back of quite smart cars, though there are more restrictions these days.

Our Blue Texels usually go to the major society sales, certainly to Worcester and Builth, where a show is held on the Sunday evening and the sale on the Monday. Over the years we've done very well with both male and female Championships, and while profitable sales are important, a major part is the camaraderie. We only meet up with certain friends, fellow sheep breeders, once or twice a year, but the overnight sales and shows, give us plenty of time to catch up and enjoy each other's company.

Last year, I saw Lanark again, for the Texel sale. On the first day Aub needed to be on sight early to inspect, so I stayed in bed with a good book, took a long hot shower, indulged in a late breakfast then asked reception to summon a taxi to take me to the sale. No point in arriving too early – contact with Aub is limited while he's inspecting.

Having studied my catalogue and marked the sheep I was interested to see, I wandered down the lines of huge cattle pens that would dwarf most sheep. Not so, when it's top class Texel lambs. Again, I'm taken by the size of these lambs, which would put ours to shame. They were probably the same weight as ours at fourteen weeks and may be smaller than ours by the time they're shearlings. They have been thoroughly prepared for this sale and will probably never again look as good as they do today. As long as one's aware of this fact, it's possible to seek out a useful lamb. Often this is one with good bloodlines which some unknown breeder has bred by artificial insemination, or a smaller lamb.

Trade was down last autumn. This could be due to the uncertainty post-Brexit or perhaps a lack of quality breeding stock. I really don't know. The occasional sheep will still make six figures, probably purchased by a syndicate or as a tax loss, but there were good sheep to be bought at sensible, even ridiculously low prices.

Lanark is the sale where every vendor brings their best lambs. Well grown, white and sparkling, with those classic black tear ducts required by all breeders. Our commercial rams sell very well at home, buyers are more interested in their growth rate and muscle depth than specific breeding, but females need to sparkle. I was searching for a ram to pass this on.

Two years earlier, we'd tried to buy a ram lamb at Worcester from an Irish breeder. Nearing the end of the sale, when most had bought and gone, his lambs made very little money. We were interested in the best lamb of his run and bid to £600. The vendor wouldn't sell at that, we went further, he still refused and the auctioneer suggested he left the ring. Aub and I discussed this ram, which had everything. To produce females like himself he was worth four figures to us but outside the ring the vendor wouldn't name a price, so sadly we had to pass him up. In all honesty, earlier in the sale he would have made twice what we were offering, but timing can make all the difference.

The same vendor had a pen of lambs at Lanark with some related breeding. I'd marked a particular one and went to have a look. Not the biggest in the pen, but just our sort. When no one was looking, I entered the pen and handled him. Small he might be, but everything I wanted was there. Good top line and backend, with silky white hair and the darkest of tear ducts. At that point Jimmy, a top Scottish breeder came into the pen.

"You like these as well, do you?" he asked, smiling. He went through and handled all four lambs. "Good enough sorts, aren't they?"

My heart sank. I agreed. Please don't like mine. We caught up on our family's health and the current state of farming and moved onto other pens. I thought I'd better have a few more to choose from.

Later that day Aub and I walked round, looking at those we'd both marked. We ran the Irish lamb out and agreed he looked straight, and did the same with several others. To my relief the Irish lamb didn't come out in the show, another from his pen did. Not surprising, the rest were all bigger than him.

Sale morning and, as usual, I kept losing Aub, with others always asking his advice. Just before it started, we ran the little Irish lamb out again and agreed he was worth a shot. I hurried back to the ring, he was soon to come in, and Jimmy was watching at the gates. The first two made good money and Jimmy still hadn't bid.

Then came mine, looking quite smart. Several put bids in before me. Not being well known to Brian, the auctioneer, I had to wave quite forcefully for him to take my bid. To my amazement the others stopped, the hammer went down and he mouthed 'Aubrey?' to me. I nodded and sat mesmerised for a moment. Jimmy bid hard for the last of the pen of lambs, securing it for considerably more than mine. Aub then reappeared, having been waylaid for discussion by another breeder.

"When's he in?" he asked. "Someone stopped me and I couldn't get away."

"I've bought him. No one else bid again."

Neither of us could believe it.

"Let's go and check we haven't missed anything, such as he's only got three legs."

"Shouldn't the inspector have noticed that?"

Back at the pen we were as pleased with him as before. Aub thought Jimmy had bought a good lamb, but we had no reason to prefer it to ours. Now all we needed was to find him a lift home. 'Easyjet' might object to him on the plane.

Three days later at Worcester, Aub suddenly decided to bid on another lamb just as it was entering the ring. We didn't need another, but this pen of top-class Scottish ram lambs was selling for next to nothing, and when the best of the consignment came in, he bought him.

Now, well set up for rams, we could look forward to some exciting lambs in the spring.

CHAPTER 30

Selling Homebred Rams

Selling our homebred rams can be quite amusing. Happy that we've ensured that our next year's crop of lambs is established, autumn is the time for selling both the homebred Texel and Blue Texel shearling rams, and the odd Charollais cross Texel that Aubrey bred in a weak moment. Most of our rams are sold direct to other farmers straight from the farm. For many this is the most satisfactory way to buy. They can see how the farm is managed, look at other stock if they wish and have a selection to choose from at various prices.

We've spent over two hours in the pens while a regular buyer tries to decide which two he really wants out of the four rams we've selected for him to choose from. I've had long-suffering wives ask me to just select the most suitable and only show those two to their husbands the following year!

New buyers can also be interesting. A couple of years ago one rang to say he'd seen the rams a neighbour had bought from us and thought he'd like to give Blue Texel's a try.

"Don't want to pay the silly sort of money he'll have paid though," the caller emphasised. Knowing his neighbour had just bought some really good shearlings from us, I assured him we had several lesser animals at very reasonable prices that would definitely do an excellent job. His neighbour has been a customer for a few years, always wanted the best, never quibbled the price and knew our rams gave him top class lambs.

Aub was busy, so I ended up selecting the rams myself. Typically, one of the remaining top, most expensive Blue rams refused to leave the others I'd picked and there was no arguing with him. When our new customer arrived, he immediately took to this big boy.

"Yes, I'm sorry," I apologised. "He insisted on coming in with these and I couldn't get him back out again, but the others are what you're looking for, I guess."

He looked through my selection then back at the big one. "He's expensive I expect." The price was almost double what I was asking for the others. "Can't go too silly, I need a Charollais as well."

By the time we'd finished negotiations he'd purchased the big Blue and two Charollais x Texels. All expensive. He was delighted with his lambs the following year and all the rams are still working well for him.

If we do sell at a livestock sale, we like to be sure there will be buyers looking for quality. Agriculture is probably the only industry where the producer has no idea what he will make of his product at the end of the day. This is particularly true of livestock markets. We all follow the agricultural press, watching for peaks and troughs in the price of sheep, be it prime or store lambs, breeding ewes or rams, but you never really know until the day. It's always better to go to a sale with a figure in mind you're happy to accept then sometimes your expectations will be exceeded.

With pedigree prime stock, we can always withdraw something that doesn't make enough money, but trade throughout has to be considered. Sometimes, when all prices are low, pedigree sheep can run up a lot of mileage and still not make any more money at a later sale. When trade is buoyant everyone seems satisfied. Buyers are a funny breed. They often prefer to pay a good price, valuing the animal more for the higher cost.

When prices are low, a livestock market can be the most depressing place on earth. Buyers don't think there's anything worth paying much for and vendors are disappointed. The air reeks of muck, dirty straw, and damp sheep. Surrounded by concrete and metal everything is grey. Men of all ages, though the majority look seventy or older, with a sprinkling of women, often younger. But this is still a man's stronghold.

If prices are poor, depression falls like a dark cloud, in deep folds. Bodies stoop lower. The quality of the stock for sale is varied, but when the auctioneer arrives at a pen of good rams, spirits rise a little. Are our as good as these? Maybe better? Who knows the buyer's thoughts? A farmer argues the bid taken wasn't what he offered. Discussion is rapid. The next pen needs selling.

By noon those alleys under cover warm up. Ammonia pervades the air. Though a cold wind blows round the outer pens, that air quality is preferable. Rain is threatening.   W e need to make it worthwhile, having reared our rams to 18 months old.

Echoes of bids from £200 to £260 permeate the mist over a nearby pen. More than twice that is sensible but today doesn't look optimistic. The auctioneer moves on. I look at the pen of rams that made such a poor price and agree they don't impress. Please let ours do better. I know ours look better. Are better. But bidders can be fickle.

If selling meat lambs, and sometimes even pedigree stock, bids can be taken in halves. Often the Welsh markets will up a bid by 50 pence. Sheep can have left the ring while bids for them are still being bandied about, and the next lot has come in. If sold in pens we usually see the conclusion of one sale pen before the auctioneer walks along the wall to the next.

The auctioneer reaches our pen and makes encouraging comments on the quality of this pen of sheep. Bidding starts high and progresses well through the sale of all six rams. Relief brings a smile to my face. They've sold well, several to buyers who know our stock and have bought in previous years. Obviously, those they've bought before have done them proud.

Markets are always cold. The only bright spot is the café and I've yet to find a market without a good café. When the children were younger it was their favourite venue on the day.

Back in the eighties, when we had our first twenty or thirty commercial sheep, I was often the one to take our lambs to market, usually with at least one child in tow, as Aub was working.

At both Gloucester and Cirencester, I recognised several old farmers who didn't appear to have stock in or be interested in buying. One, a tallish man with little hair and buck teeth, another short, rotund and a little better dressed than the first. Being young and naive, I wondered why they were always there, following the line of sheep being sold. It's only in later years I appreciated the market was their lifeline, a way to stave off loneliness and mental health issues by contact with others of their fraternity. Farming can be a lonely lifestyle. These men were probably retired farm-workers with little in common with their neighbours, just seeking to stay within friends of the farming community.

"Hey, watch it." A kerfuffle erupted behind me as I wandered along the walkway between the pens.

"Watch him," an irate drover shouted in my direction. I turned and realised four-year-old Mark who had been trotting happily behind me, was slipping the chains off the pens, releasing lambs into the walkway as he went. His small pink face looked at me then back at the man shouting. I managed to secure the last of the pens, grabbed Mark's hand and pulled him towards me. Chaos reigned for a few minutes but we were gone, the promise of a drink and biscuit at the café brightening the crumpled face near to tears.

"Don't worry, they'll sort it out," I said. I presumed playing with the chains was an outlet for boredom. Sitting at the café table with drinks and a cheese roll for lunch, I was soon enlightened.

"There were too many lambs in those pens," said Mark. "They needed more room."

A genuine plan to disrupt the market on welfare issues? I kept a better eye on him when we returned to see our lambs sold.

Heather and Mark at a show. Mark must have been happier with the size of the pen here

Chapter 31

Richard's Parties

For all farmers, Autumn is the time for celebration and giving thanks for a successful season. The corn harvest and straw are safely in, and the hay has been in the barns since July. Sheep farmers have sold some lambs and we have sold most of our breeding rams. The village church holds its Harvest Festival service, usually followed by a traditional harvest supper: ham supplied by a local pig farmer, potatoes and salad followed by apple pie and cream. Delicious.

Harvest parties are about unexpected friendships too. We moved to Througham in the seventies with no idea of our illustrious neighbours, but were soon great friends with them all. We could go weeks without catching sight of Richard, the owner of the large farm at Upper Througham, aware he was probably in London. Then suddenly he'd appear, bombing around the fields in his shiny blue, top of the range tractor, radio blaring, smiling from ear to ear. Upper Througham was Richard's safety valve. A high flyer in the city, with fingers in many pies, we saw him at his most relaxed (apart from being terrorised by Satan - see *If Clouds Were Sheep*).

Whatever cultivation he was meant to be doing was usually done at such speed one of his employees would have to redo it later, but that wasn't important. His farm was his 'fun palace' and he loved it.

He'd made many changes to the original farmhouse, but it wasn't until his first harvest supper party that we really appreciated what a wonderful home he'd created. Way ahead of his time in design, the ground floor was completely open plan. The beamed room was immense: a huge dining area with long oak table and chairs, merging into a sitting room with massive leather settees and armchairs. These faced a line of glass doors, which took in the panorama of the Cotswold valley and undulating distant hills. Views to die for. The colour scheme was a blend of soft whites and greyish fawn against the faded oak beams and, with a highly sophisticated system, music followed you everywhere.

That fantastic harvest supper, with foods we'd only dreamt of, was Richard's gift to all his local farming friends, and he had many. He was not the usual aloof Londoner who came down to the country for occasional visits, but a major part of Througham and the surrounding area. A member of Sheepscombe cricket team along with Fred, the captain, he could be seen drinking with poet Frank Mansell and writer Laurie Lee.

But the real highlights for us were his regular parties, to which we were often invited. We met many famous faces, if only we could remember who, and wandering home late from one such party, slightly inebriated, we tried to place the nice chap we'd been talking to for ages, who'd been really interested in sheep farming. It took us about two weeks to realise it was Noel Edmunds.

On other occasions, Aub and I were invited for drinks and supper with the arrangement we'd babysit the small children while their very bohemian parents and others moved on to a night club in Bath, or a gallery opening. This was the era of hallucinogenic drugs and children called Moonbeam or Sunlight, not that it made them any less endearing. Most came with nannies so our involvement was minimal. We were just local backup in case anything went wrong. It never did.

Richard had the most iconic friends from both the music and film industry visiting. Members of the Rolling Stones were occasionally seen traipsing across his fields, and Bill Wyman had bought a local property. Once I scowled hard at Oliver Tobias, my current pinup of the time, as he raced past our gate. It was a straight piece of lane and he drove a beast of a car.

"He'll run the ducks over," I said to Aub. Our duck families often crossed the lane to the field opposite. "You'll have to put a sign: *'SLOW, Ducks Crossing'.*"

"Mmm, not sure how well that'll go down, they're eating Richard's corn."

It was rumoured Richard had connections with Roddy Llewelyn. We saw many of the music and film set in passing, but didn't glimpse Roddy with his royal connection. Musician Mike Oldfield was another who discovered the hidden secrets of our beautiful Cotswold valley. He is actually quoted as saying *'We wouldn't have Tubular Bells without drugs'!* I loved that piece, but found Moonlight Shadow particularly poignant. I can't say we were bosom friends with Mike, but became great friends with Paul, his sound mixer, and wife Claire.

She enjoyed bringing their young children to see the sheep and I was equally fascinated by the vast sound system in the barn. I remember this as wall to wall synthesisers and a quadraphonic mixer which Paul would demonstrate. The sounds were amazing. One of Mike Oldfield's hits 'Incantations' was actually recorded in that barn at Througham Slad.

Perhaps it was the artistic aura of the valley that inspired us all. While I cannot claim to be in the league of those mentioned, I did first start to write in that idyllic setting.

It's easy to feel inspired in this setting

CHAPTER 32

No Room for Sentiment

On 3rd September 1981 the passing of Lulubell went without the world noticing. No flags were lowered; there were few mourners, but I missed her terribly.

I missed her silly brown face and curly hairstyle that always presented itself in the bucket whenever food was in the offing. Her raucous "baa" was heard above all the others as I approached the sheep shed. The familiar way she could run across the field and chew at my jacket pockets in search of sheep nuts.

She'd arrived in the autumn some six years before, an old ewe then. Part of a "flying flock" we'd intended to lamb down and sell for slaughter once the lambs were weaned. I still have wonderful memories of taking delivery of those twenty Mule ewes late one September evening, thrilled to have eventually moved into the realms of proper sheep farmers.

Mules are the cross breeding of Swaledale and Blue Leicester parentage, much used in the North of England and much sought after in the South. It was almost dark when we unloaded so it wasn't until the following day we realised one didn't match the others and obviously had a fair percentage of Teeswater blood judging by her curly fleece. She was a Masham.

They'd travelled down to Gloucestershire from Cumberland, possibly on the open top deck of a three-deck sheep wagon, a practice now banned, and were pleasantly surprised on arrival to discover far better grazing than they'd been used to in the hills.

It soon became apparent that the curly coated sheep had been someone's pet, and possibly a good few years ago, a bottled lamb. She knew the sight of a bucket or bag of feed and came rushing up to me regularly for titbits. She had to have a name. How Lulubell, (Lulu for short), originated I really can't remember, but it seemed to suit her.

She was one of seven ewes who ignored our rather handsome Suffolk ram, for which he took the blame. When they all lambed earlier than anticipated we realised they'd arrived in-lamb.

A complete novice, I was delighted when Lulu lambed first, and with triplets. I checked they were all alright and sucking well and thought what a good start to our lambing.

Four days later I was reduced to tears when Lulu's biggest lamb died for no apparent reason, though it was probably from lack of milk. I now know this is not unusual in the sheep world: lambs and sheep prefer to die if living involves any real effort, but this was my first loss when in sole charge. Hindsight and experience are invaluable. It's doubtful an old ewe like Lulu would have produced enough milk for three lambs. Her remaining children would run up and down the line of ewes feeding at the troughs, taking a quick suck at each until they were kicked away. The second year she also had triplets and lost one, even though I'd been much more prepared with top-up bottles.

The following autumn Aubrey was offered what appeared to be a good job in Oxfordshire, and our move involved the sale of our small flock. Not Lulu. I couldn't send her to market, so she and another ewe she was great friends with, went to live with Claire in Througham Slad. This time Lulu had a Welsh cross ram lamb as a husband and safely delivered two lambs. Both lambs were topped-up with bottles, as by then Lulu really shouldn't have been in lamb and was unlikely to be producing any milk.

The Oxfordshire job turned out to be unsuccessful. After nine months we returned to Gloucestershire to take up a new job and re-instate our flock.

Amid many protests from Aub, I was re-united with Lulu. "Our sheep are supposed to be profit-making, she's far too old to produce lambs." She certainly was showing her age. and was showing problems with arthritis. She came back to us with no front teeth, not that it affected her eating powers or caused lack of condition, but she was glad to come into the sheep shed out of the inclement weather and be fed on nuts.

And then, surprising us all, three weeks after everyone had lambed she again produced two strong, healthy lambs, who were bottled from the start.

She had a wonderful summer with the flock. Then the damp atmosphere aggravated her rheumatics and arthritis and I had to admit it was pure selfishness to allow her to remain in that condition. The matter was humanely dealt with at home, without causing her any fear or confusion. She'd had at least five years longer than the average commercial ewe and at a rough calculation must have reached the grand age of thirteen or fourteen. But I did miss her. Although often reminded there is no room for sentiment in farming, I wouldn't want to do it without.

CHAPTER 33

To Russia, With Love

When your children become adults, they have this power to take over your life in a very different way – steering you in the right direction and taking full charge of events. This became quite obvious when we went to London to complete our visa applications for a trip to Russia.

When we first mentioned to our son Mark that we were going to an agricultural exhibition in Moscow he was very envious, saying it was one place he'd love to visit. Then the opportunity arose for him to come with us, representing his own flock of Corinium Blue Texel sheep, so he jumped at it.

However, I soon found that visiting Russia was not going to be straight forward. To gain visas, we, or rather I, would have to complete some long and taxing paperwork, take it personally to the Russian Visa office in London and also have our fingerprints taken. At this point I was visualising the old-fashioned detective films, with fingers pushed into black ink and pressed on paper. This is now done electronically.

The day started well, although the Blue Texels in the twelve-acre decided overnight they'd devour all their hay even though

Aub had stuffed their rack full the previous evening. Feeding them twice wasn't really in my timetable. Still, with Mark T, who helps on the farm, we managed to finish by 9:15am, with time to change and pick son Mark up at 10am, to catch the London train from Stroud.

The train was a few minutes late, but we reached Paddington at twelve, as expected. Here the first slight disagreement occurred when Mark assured us that he'd researched the underground and we needed the Hammersmith and City line, but we appeared to have left the station in the wrong direction. He was obviously of the opinion that I had no idea where we were going, although I had sorted all this out. I pointed out that the Circle line would also take us to the Barbican, so we walked quickly towards that platform. This was when I realised that my dress sense had let me down. Thinking that I should smarten myself up a bit to go to the big city, I'd chosen my heeled boots instead of my everyday flat shoes. Consequently, I trailed ten feet behind the men. These boots were not the easiest to walk fast in, especially when you spend most of the day in wellies.

"We'll get on this one," said Mark, with authority. A train was already standing on the platform.

"Are you sure?" I asked, not being certain it was a Circle line train.

Yes, he was definite, until they announced it was the District line. We got off. The next one arrived just a minute later and specified its destination on the front.

"Could have got that last one and changed at Edgeware Road," he said, with great authority, once he'd studied the overhead map. I agreed, but it seemed more sense to stay on the same train. We stopped at several stations along the route.

"Faringdon?" asked Aub. "We going the right way, or back to Oxford?"

Mark and I ignored him, passing through Faringdon and getting off at Barbican. Outside the station we had the next slight disagreement.

"This way," said our newly-appointed leader, striding off to the right with Aub. Still tottering along behind them, they did at least wait for me to cross the road at speed, obeying the pedestrian lights, Aub pulling me along to make sure I kept up.

"I'm not sure this is right," I said. "I thought we'd turn left out of the station."

"Well, we can go that way if you want. We'll probably get run over crossing one of these roads, so we might as well keep going." Mark was obviously not impressed.

"Let me have the map I printed off." It was with all the Visa paperwork in the laptop bag, now in Aub's charge. Mark quickly attempted to get Google maps up, but found he had no signal. This was when I stopped a lady and asked if she knew where Gee Street was. Sadly, she was not local, but she rapidly gained access to Google maps. Left looked the way we should be going, though Mark and Aub were not really convinced. Then the row started.

"Don't ask people the way," Mark was furious.

"That's a typical man approach. We're lost! Someone else may know the way, but no, we mustn't ask. What is your problem?"

This brought back memories of my parents coming to visit us at Througham, long before anyone had satnav. Commenting that they were later than expected, my mother quietly mentioned they'd been through Caudle Green three times.

She whispered confidentially to me, "We were obviously lost and did pass a couple of people, but your father refused to stop to ask the way. Men don't, do they? We carried on driving in circles for another half an hour before we found a road that resembled anything on the map"

I've always wondered how they'd got to Caudle Green in the first place, but once there, could relate to the fact that the signposts would not have mentioned Miserden let alone Througham.

With that memory fresh in my mind, I retrieved my map from Aub. "Yes, this is the right way. Barbican's on our right, so it should be just up here."

It was now raining quite heavily, but what's the point of having good weather and being in London? We carried on in the direction I felt was correct, me still tottering behind, catching up with them when they felt we were lost again. We all studied the map and thought the side road we needed should be on the opposite side of the main road, but to clarify matters, and annoy them further, I shot into a stationers where the gentleman behind the counter confirmed it was just along the road on the other side.

While they were waiting for me Mark had gained signal and Google maps and agreed it was where I was saying, but assured me that we'd approached from the wrong direction as we'd have to go right round the building to gain access.

"I think we got off at the wrong station," he announced. "We should have got off at Faringdon. This is miles round."

After two more hazardous road crossings we found Gee Street, and just a few yards up the entrance to the Visa Application Centre. I wasn't sure what map Mark had been looking at but felt it unwise to query.

Inside we were greeted by a tall, thick set, definitely Russian gentleman who issued us with a number and indicated for us to wait on the row of chairs, opposite a line of desks manned by very efficient looking girls. The last number they were dealing with was 127. We were 144, but were not waiting too long. It was interesting seeing which people took more time to be dealt with.

"Shouldn't take us long, will it, Mum? You've filled out all the applications and we've got the photos." I knew Mark was aiming to go somewhere nice for lunch.

I hoped he was right. Our photographs had to be recent. Glancing down at mine, taken the day before, I wondered why I always seemed to pull an awful face in those photo booths. For the past six years I'd thought my passport picture looked as though I'd suffered a stroke, on reflection I almost looked glamorous, compared to yesterday's attempt. Perhaps I always look like that. The reflection I see in the mirror is totally different from how others see me.

The buzzer indicated it was our turn and en masse we trooped up to the desk.

"I'll do mine first, "I said, "then if anything's wrong I can sort it."

Oh, how blasé can one be? Looking down page one the clerk pointed out that I'd incorrectly filled in the organisation who had invited us to Russia, so to go to the computers available to alter it. No, I couldn't just write it in. Anyone could do that and it was an official document. Even though she could see me do it and I could sign it, but no.

"Right, they'll all be wrong," I said, and we all trouped over to the three computers, all in use at that moment, to queue for our position. Having first given thanks that I had put my other glasses in the case, when a computer became free, I sat in front of it and looked at the screen in horror, all memory of what to do leaving me. It wouldn't have been such a panic if I'd just asked the young woman who was there to help, but no, Mark took charge again, asking me for all my log ins, so I could find the old paperwork. I didn't think I needed this, but couldn't remember any of my passwords anyway. I keep them in a book at home.

"How do you log in away from home?" he asked, his sense of humour having totally left him by now.

"I don't, unless it's on my laptop. Then it just comes up."

While Mark backed away to ring his office, where he keeps a list of my passwords in case I lose them, the clerk directed me to the page I'd expected to use. My request to open my application was rejected, saying there was not one of that number. It was then I realised I'd made the application 32 days previously and they only save them for 30 days. I would just have to complete the entire forms again, for all three of us, instead of altering a small bit on page one.

I couldn't believe it. We had intended to do this before

Christmas, then when that failed, come up on the 7th January, until I discovered the centre was closed from 1st – 8th, for the Russian Orthodox holiday, so here we were on 14th with no saved copies.

Originally, it had taken me about four hours to complete my first application, followed by a two-hour stint for each of Aub's and Mark's, as by then I had more idea of what I was doing. OK, I had all the information in front of me, all I had to do was copy it, all five pages of each, with the small alteration. Just a pity that the printed form was not generated in the same order as the questions on the screen, all of which required the dates of birth of every single relation, dead or alive and dates and places we have visited outside the UK in the past ten years.

My typing skills are nowhere near as proficient as Mark's, but he refrained from comment, simply reading dates and passport numbers to me, which did speed the process up a bit. Two hours later, praying all had been completed correctly, we were back at the desk ten minutes after they closed. Eventually, a different, efficient young lady checked things through, photocopied bank statements and, pointing out we would need the visas done by the more costly express service, charged just over £500 for the three. At this point I was thinking – is it all worth it?

Payment made, then the fingerprints, which actually only needed our fingers and thumbs placed on a screen. Aub had trouble fitting his enormous farmer's hands in the space allowed and I caused problems with fingers that have been broken by animals in the past, not lying flat to show the finger prints correctly, but eventually we were sorted.

The walk back to the Barbican station was a lot quicker than our outward journey, knowing where we were going this time, then through to Paddington just in time to catch the last train our day ticket permitted us to use that evening. Our meal out ended up as burger and chips at Paddington. A fun day was had by all, ha ha. I just hoped the visas would come through with no more problems.

CHAPTER 34

Moscow

Well, we made it to Moscow. This was as part of an agricultural delegation, but I think we were just happy to be visiting, whether sales materialised or not. Having been told to wear something warm, of course Moscow was having its mildest winter since records began. While freezing outside, but not minus twenty, the hotel was boiling. It was hot at the airport and on the flight. Cooler at the exhibition centre, but we were never cold.

Our taxi took us from Vnukovo airport to our hotel and the exhibition at Strogino. There had been snow, but driving was not in any way restricted, our taxi changing lanes every few minutes and keeping up a steady speed of far-too-fast. Interestingly, I deduced that Russia must have an excellent freight service on the railways as we saw very few lorries on the roads. However, when we thought about it afterwards, a lot of freight must travel by sea as Moscow isn't a great distance from St Petersburg.

The Russians we met seemed rather sullen with grey complexions and didn't give the impression of being happy people. In fairness, perhaps the older generation haven't had a lot to be happy about, but some gave us very funny looks if we smiled at them. On the flight I studied a few words of Russian. I feel it's polite to be able to say a little in the country's language, even if it's just 'please' and 'thank you.'

Our first night's meal at the small restaurant attached to the Hilton was awful; the little they had left on the menu was lukewarm. A very liquid mash potato was served with the majority of dishes. Although we found two far better traditional restaurants later in the week, I still wouldn't suggest these were a culinary triumph.

We were on site at the exhibition by nine in the morning and by eleven it was still very quiet. Our team included Aub and me, selling Texels, Mark with Blue Texels and several other breeders. Carroll and Jonathan with Charollais sheep, Gregor selling almost every breed under the sun, most being some form of Texel cross and Chris, I think, was marketing pigs. We had two young women interpreting as well as Ury, a friend from Ukraine.

The exhibition complex had numerous halls, but only one being used and a small one at that. There was a little interest in the sheep, but we were tucked away at the back, hidden behind a large tractor and feed wagon, which was certainly causing more interest than we were. There were some livestock on display, but even these took some searching for, as they were in a small side hall.

Lunch was interesting. We took one of our interpreters along, as the prospect of discussing a menu in Russian looked daunting. Even with her help I obviously took too long making my choice. She told me I must to hurry up as the lady behind the counter was saying there was a long queue. My selection left much to be desired and I decided to try something different the next day!

The show finished at six each day. It was 5.30 before we had any real interest: a gentleman who wanted to start up a sheep farm. Apparently, he had money but just needed facts and figures, which we promised to sort out on our return to UK. He was obviously very interested because he emailed me later that evening.

That night Ury took us to a traditional Russian restaurant, where the food far surpassed the previous evening. Photographs on the restaurant wall showed Putin, Gorbachev and Michelle Obama all dining there at different times. The menu was interesting. Bear featured in a number of dishes, and Aub wished he hadn't chosen Elk, which proved a little chewy! The borsch was delicious and I opted for the safety of pork.

Day two and considerably more people attended the show, but still few arriving at our stand during the morning. A visit from the Representative for International Trade, who was a very pretty petite Chinese woman, and a photoshoot added a bit of interest. The afternoon proved more productive and we left around four thirty to travel the hour and a half to central Moscow, for the Ambassador's cocktail party.

Immediately opposite the Kremlin, on the far side of the river Sofia, the Ambassador's residence was once the home of a major Ukrainian sugar baron. The guards outside were very pleasant and jovial, quite different from those we saw in Kiev a couple of years ago. In fact, there was nothing obviously threatening about Russia, other than learning the second part of a small document given out at the airport, where they kept one part, was essential to show when we left Moscow, otherwise we might have to stay. Mark immediately felt he was the most suitable one to look after these and I didn't argue. If anyone lost them, don't let it be me.

The interior of the building was amazing. Huge tapestries hung on the walls over the stairs, and paintings of outstanding quality in the main rooms. One wonderful panelled room had a ceiling decorated to show people looking down at you from a terrace. Quite incredible.

After a rather strange presentation from the Russian members of JCB, we, the UK Agricultural Trade delegation were introduced. This was followed by a delightful cocktail party with canapés to die for, and cocktails sponsored by a Scottish whisky company, whose name escapes me, but I was hooked on their Whisky sours. We managed to meet and discuss trade and movement logistics with a number of Embassy members, who followed up our discussions with emails. These gave us hope that, should we wish to sell them sheep, protocols could be put in place to transport them direct from UK to Russia.

Jonathan was feeling unwell, so he and wife Carroll decided to return to the hotel at around nine o'clock. I went with them. After five whisky sours, I didn't feel the need to accompany Aub, Mark and others on their night trip around Moscow. I thought their outing would probably end up as a pub crawl, but not so. A fairly sober Aub woke me at 2 am having forgotten to take his room key with him! Drinking had been limited and his worse complaint was they hadn't been able to buy fish and chips anywhere.

By now I was trying my few words of Russian, though I had to memorise something similar in English to remember the Russian word. My first and most useful word was pronounced 'spasiba', which means 'thank you'. I had to think of 'spicy bar', then I got it relatively understandable, until after the whiskeys. 'Eta' meaning 'this', I could remember and teamed this up with 'harashow' which means good, just remember 'horror show'. I got quite good at pointing to pictures of the sheep and using this small phrase. This was after I remembered 'privet' and said 'priveeyet' which is 'Hi'. That, I regret was my limit of studying the Russian language, but I did use 'spasiba' extensively, feeling very proud of myself.

We may have sold sheep, we may not, but we enjoyed a visit to Red Square at night. We watched Russian dancers give a display and visited the tomb of the unknown soldier, which is guarded day and night. It was snowing as we walked alongside the Kremlin and admired the spires of Saint Basil's Cathedral just as any tourist would. Still celebrating the Orthodox Christmas period, everything was lit up to the extreme, with no regard to energy efficiency. Shops were open late into the evening and the largest mall, Gum, the equivalent to Harrods, had everything imaginable for sale. One window hosted a huge display of caviar, some at prices only the oligarchs could afford. Quite magical to realise where the farming life can take you.

Heather and Porty (left) riding off the opposition

CHAPTER 35

Heather, Polo, New Zealand

Some of Heather's escapades in New Zealand came as a slight surprise to me when I asked her for memories of her visit. She was eighteen, hated farming and school and had reached an age where she was going to have to decide what to do for a living. The invitation to spend six months abroad playing polo had been rapidly taken up by her and Diana from the Cotswold 2nd Team. They'd been playing together throughout the summer, but they weren't great friends at that point. This soon changed.

As the departure date approached, Heather grew more apprehensive of the trip. I did catch her packing four big boxes of Tampax, until I persuaded her there were shops in New Zealand. Things also improved after Nick, who would be her host, rang and said if he missed the girls at the airport, they should stand outside McDonalds and he'd find them.

"What! They have McDonalds in New Zealand?"

Heather was now excited and relieved. I think, up until then, she'd thought we were sending her to a third world country.

"Six months away will do her a world of good," Aub said. "Hopefully she'll return with a clearer outlook on life."

13th October 1995, their flight left from Heathrow at around ten in the morning. Luggage was sorted, with polo sticks carefully labelled and sent with their suitcases to the hold. Then the goodbyes, which ended up with both Heather and me in tears, while Diana and her mother looked on in astonishment. On the plane Heather explained to Dee the furthest she'd been away on her own was a weekend trip to Sidmouth with a cousin, and that she'd never flown before. Diana was amazed; she'd been sent to boarding school aged eight and flown half way round the world with her parents and friends.

Just after I arrived home, the phone rang.

"Where are you?" asked Mary. "I thought we were going to the Cob show at Northleach. Shall I pick you up?" This had been arranged for weeks and I'd completely forgotten about it.

"Oh, no. I can't possibly go anywhere. Heather's in the air, flying to New Zealand."

"Of course, but how does that affect things?"

"I need to be here. I can't go away." I don't think I've ever been so unreasonable in my life. I was devastated. I'd put my daughter on a plane for a twenty-four-hour flight, and completely gone to pieces.

Aub took over the phone. "I don't think she'll be coming with you, Mary, you wouldn't want her either. She's having a very funny five minutes, which I think may go on until our darling daughter arrives in Auckland. I honestly don't know what difference it makes where Sue is, but as you can imagine, there's no reasoning to be done."

I can't remember whether I felt distraught the entire time Heather was flying, but I did feel an absolute idiot afterwards. Anyhow, it caused Mary and me great amusement on future trips.

Heather rang me the day they arrived; horrified that Nick had made them clean out a really filthy horsebox, full of muck, to ensure they didn't fall asleep from jetlag.

"The place we're living in is a shed! You'd be appalled. And Nick thinks because Dad's a sheep farmer, that I love working with sheep! Wrong. I hate them. He made us go down to the creek and pull out a dead one, and its legs came off. Gross."

Obviously, things weren't going quite as planned. Nick had also filled their freezer with lamb, which Heather had always refused to eat. When she told him this, he said he'd 'throw in a few chucks then'.

Then came the phone call: Heather hated it and wanted to come home.

"We'll sort something out darling," I started to say, until Aub took the phone.

"You're there for six months and you're jolly lucky, so I would make the most of it!" he hung up.

This, of course, was by far the best reaction and from then on, she did get on with it. I was reminded of Hello Muddah, Hello Faddah, the Camp Grenada song by Allen Sherman.

Look it up if you don't know it and listen right to the end.

Heather had turned down my offer of some basic cookery lessons before she went, so it came as a surprise when she phoned for a lasagne recipe. Apparently, she did manage to make a reasonable one, then dropped it getting it out of the oven, so they had a takeaway.

Rapidly she learnt the skills of grooming for two patrons as well as playing polo herself. She'd come a long way from the days of grooming for Paddy. Some of her ponies weren't great. Gull would nip her if given half a chance and Silk took off as soon as she put her foot in the stirrup. Terry was her favourite. However, he gave her the fright of her life at one of the big matches. She'd tacked him up earlier then when she tightened his girth he collapsed on the floor as though dead. She was to discover, if she didn't tighten the girth very carefully, he could do this on a regular basis.

Life seemed to bounce from polo grounds to bars. Bills from the Dairy and Liquor King eventually followed her home for us to pay!

"Morning tea after riding out our first sets was my favourite time," Heather told me. "Nick would bring out our letters. You'd write most days and tell me what you were all doing at home. It seems strange to look back – no Facetime or mobiles. On Christmas Day we were on the verandas and it was so hot we spent the whole time looking for ice. I rang you in the evening and it was still Christmas Eve, you were making mince pies and I really felt homesick again."

A lovely surprise for the girls was when JonP, from Edgeworth Polo Club, arrived just before Christmas. He'd rung to let us know he was going and could he take any presents, which was great.

Heather and Dee, as Diana was now affectionately called, discovered at eighteen they weren't allowed in NZ pubs and needed a patron with them. Living with several older girls that wasn't a problem, although their behaviour obviously was. Jane, a straight-talking Australian polocrosse champion, who took no messing, said: "you two need to stop being so stuck up and just muck in, or nobody's going to like you." Her sound advice went home and Jane became a very dear friend.

There were many highlights Heather relayed to me at the time, and more I've found out about since. I'm sure there are others I won't hear. There were party invitations from all the top players, something the girls loved. Dee was a polo fanatic and knew all the players names and handicaps.

On their return to the UK the two girls immediately bonded with their other team mate Sophie again, who was still at school. Somehow they managed to smuggle her out of Westonbirt for several polo parties at both Kirtlington and Windsor. I'm not sure whether Aub would class that as returning with a clearer outlook on life, but polo certainly gave Heather some amazing, lifelong friends.

Now, twenty eight years on, they're all married with families, and have settled in their chosen careers. Heather's wonderful way with people has led her to top jobs in both recruitment and HR, her caring and thoughtful attitude of much greater value than academic achievement.

CHAPTER 36

Italian Connection

There are always deaths within families. Some we are prepared for. Others, like my uncle dying in early March almost ten years ago, come as a shock. For many years we had lacked communication, but made contact again when my mother, his sister died back in 1988. I felt the duty of keeping in touch had now fallen to me, but rapidly found it a distinct pleasure, not an obligation.

Ken was a blast from the past; an uncle I'd known well as a small child but lost track of after his marriage – although I was the naughty bridesmaid they found stuck in a tree at his wedding reception!

My memory of him when I was younger was of a smart young man, black hair, or almost black, swept back, possibly slightly balding in the centre. I'd almost describe him as dapper.

He was a gem when I was a child. One of my birthday presents from him, when I was barely six or seven, was a fantastic metal tractor, blue and orange, about 12 inches high. At the time we lived in a top floor flat, which in itself ranged over three floors and I delighted in tying a piece of string to this tractor and taking it everywhere with me, up and down the stairs. Giving due to my parents, I believe they tolerated the noise for quite a while, before my mother suggested I kept it on one floor to avoid damaging it. A subtle suggestion. Ken also handmade me a tiny leather saddle for a later birthday, which I still have. Yes, ours was a good relationship.

Mum had kept in touch with Ken throughout their lives and on her death I wanted to take over the mantel of keeping in touch, especially after Ken's wife Ivy died.

Ken was an avid writer. On clearing his bungalow, we discovered first proofs of letters he had written to The News at 9, as it was then, disagreeing with their point of view. There were copies of his original letters to Prince Charles and replies from the royal secretary. His letters to me were epistles. Many foolscap pages, handwritten in a beautiful scrawl, but tortuous to read. Though read I did – the content was of such interest.

News of his death was heralded by the arrival of a police car and two officers approaching the front door. Being a typical farmer's wife, my first thought was – where's Aub put the guns?

Mostly they are secured away in the gun cabinet, but I've tripped over one in the hall on more than one occasion, after Aub has rushed out to shoot crows. Fortunately this train of thought didn't give me time to consider whether the police were here to tell me that Aub or one of the children had had an accident.

It transpired that Ken, at the age of 87, had been preparing his breakfast, when he'd remembered it was dustbin day.

Leaving his breakfast cooking, he'd taken his rubbish down the drive from his bungalow to the end of the farm track, returning to find the kitchen on fire. Not a man to be put off by this, he'd grabbed the hosepipe attached to the outside tap and was busy attempting to put the fire out when the postman arrived and dragged him from the burning house. He called the ambulance. Sadly, Ken had inhaled far too much smoke to survive, but at 87, and a very private man in general, I really cannot believe he could have coped with prolonged hospitalisation or staying away from his lovely home, which had been badly damaged.

It was sheer coincidence that the police contacted me. Over the previous Christmas period, when I tried ringing Ken several times and receiving no reply, I'd become worried and contacted the farmer whose track Ken shared, explaining who I was. This gentleman kindly went to check on Ken then rang me back. He'd knocked on the door, couldn't make Ken hear, but saw him in his chair, happily listening to very loud classical music. He must have kept my phone number.

As Ken's only living relative – he had no children – it was left to Aub and me to sort everything out in his West Wales house, which I was later to discover was now ours. Still at the tail end of lambing and having both suffered a stomach bug, it took a few days to arrange our trip to Pembrokeshire.

The police had organised a local builder to secure the property, but it was still a shock when we arrived. The inside was dark from the boarded windows and black from smoke damage. The smell was foul. Feeling fit and healthy, we'd have struggled to stay there a whole day, but both still feeling rough, we left for the bed and breakfast after a couple of hours, to shower and collapse into armchairs. The second day we made contact with the funeral directors, whom the police had instructed, and discussed arrangements. I was a little confused to find that they hadn't arranged Ivy's funeral, since often when one half of a couple dies, the other makes contingency plans for their own demise.

We removed the boards from parts of the windows so a little daylight shone in and continued sorting, but the building was surrounded by lines of huge dark Leylandi, growing right up to the walls, casting dark shadows and cutting out a lot of the light. The kitchen had melted and the hallway was black from smoke damage, but the fire itself seemed to have then retired to the roof. The sitting room obviously hadn't changed from the last time Ken sat in there. The bedrooms, all badly blackened, were piled high with cardboard boxes and books and nowhere to sleep. Eventually it was possible to make out a bed, totally covered in boxes and packaging. This was when we realised that the hub of my uncle's life was spent between his sitting room and the kitchen, where judging by the remains, he'd lived on tinned pies.

His sitting room consisted of a comfortable upright chair with a tartan blanket draped over it, a small table with writing equipment and remotes for his music centre and television and piles of books stacked virtually from floor to ceiling. A small narrow passageway led to the hallway, kitchen and bathroom.

"Crikey, where do we start?" I asked, suddenly appalled at the extent of the mess.

"We'd better try to sort through any paperwork, I guess,"

said Aub. "You've no idea of a solicitor or bank or anything, have you?"

"No. There was no reason to discuss anything like that with him. I'd like to be sure the funeral directors are the ones we should be using. I wonder how we find out who did Ivy's funeral. It's likely he made some arrangement then for a joint plot. I could ring all the other funeral directors in Cardigan."

"Not from here you can't. There's no mobile signal and the phones burnt out. Let's start in the dining room, there's a desk with drawers."

An obvious starting point, this was the one room we could enter without fighting our way between boxes, though it was cluttered with books and papers. The fire hadn't reached this room, but the heat had broken the windows and other glassware, so we proceeded with care. After several fruitless hours, a mound of paperwork, balancing precariously on top of a glass cabinet, fell onto my head scattering envelopes and official looking papers in all directions.

"Wow, this gives a solicitor's name," I said, excited by my find. In the middle of bank statements and other paperwork we discovered a grey foolscap file tied with pink ribbon giving details of Ivy's cremation and the arrangements made for Ken. "I felt sure he'd have sorted something out, he was so efficient."

Aub and I were sitting opposite each other on wooden dining room chairs. Thumbing through some papers, he'd found a copy of the deeds and Ken's will.

"Time to take a break and go into Cardigan to see the solicitor."

What a lovely man the solicitor was, helping us from there on to sort out the change in funeral directors and untangling a web of bank accounts. We discovered the property had been left jointly to my father and me, as my father had died a few years previously it would be ours.

We decided that Ken's funeral arrangements must take priority. We needed to muster forces from the rest of the family to stay for a couple of days after the funeral and help clear the house. We still had a few ewes lambing so couldn't stay much longer at that point. The new funeral directors pointed us in the direction of the vicar who had dealt with Ivy's funeral and a date was arranged. Mark, Heather and her fiancé Kevin were all aiming to attend and stay to help with the clear up. Mark's wife, Kate, would stay home with baby Toby.

Back at our own home briefly, I had a sudden thought, as happens at night, when the mind has time to process – I felt sure Ken had told me he'd become a Catholic. I grabbed a sweatshirt and crept downstairs to rummage through the pile of letters he'd sent me over the years. Writing had been one of his great joys, he had filled me in on many details of his life and I remembered his fantasy love affair with a beautiful Italian girl.

As a child Ken had suffered quite seriously from rheumatic fever, hence his national service in the army was totally deskbound. This hadn't stopped him travelling within Europe and for a while he'd been based in Scala, near Ravello, in Northern Italy, where this friendship had evolved. From his letters I gauged that the desire for a relationship far outstripped the actual probability. Mainly, I think, because Ken had been so shy it had taken him months to make his approaches and once he'd gathered his courage, his time was limited with her before a transfer back to London. But his feelings had been real enough. He described an equally shy but responsive girl, the daughter of the mayor, who was working alongside Ken in his office. Obviously beautiful, certainly in his eyes: 'her dusky complexion and river of black hair framing soft brown eyes and the sweetest of smiles'.

Ken left northern Italy, never to return, and possibly spent the rest of his life regretting it. How close the relationship came to reality I'll never know, but in one of his later letters he wrote, 'How could I, a common English soldier, ask the mayor for his daughter's hand in marriage?', then went on to say he would always regret not taking retirement from the army at that point, which he could have done and stayed there. It was for this lady's sake he had taken the vows of the Catholic church, which was now causing me to panic.

On our next visit to Cardigan we arranged to see the local Roman Catholic priest, who was brilliant. There was me trying to explain that we had everything set up and had now remembered Ken had specific beliefs and hoped his funeral could still be held when arranged and the priest smiled; a smile that lit his face. This charming middle-aged man that I'd been slightly terrified of meeting assured me he would check his diary, which he did, and everything could go ahead on the same date.

"We don't want a lot of waving of incense and all that stuff," I started to say as Aub scowled at me. "Sorry, I just don't think Ken would have wanted a big do," I finished lamely.

Again, our lovely priest beamed at me. "I understand exactly what you mean. We can go over the top at times, can't we?"

We then agreed on music. I found the title of a piece of classical music Ken liked, and that with one hymn fitted the bill.

On the day, the small congregation of our close family, the neighbouring farmer who had contacted me and the garage man who repaired Ken's car, made a small gathering with the undertakers in the tiny chapel. The classical piece played as the coffin came in; the short service was led by my lovely Catholic priest and then came the hymn.

I remember this every time I watch *Love Actually*, when Hugh Grant as Prime Minister has to sing *Good King Wenceslas* and his Welsh driver joins in with his deep baritone voice.

As we, the family, began the hymn as boldly as we could, we appeared to have a complete Welsh male voice choir join us. Still singing we looked at each other in amazement. It was quite incredible. The undertaker's team, who had boosted our numbers, certainly boosted our singing.

All were invited to lunch at the small hotel where we were staying for a couple of nights. We headed for the beach that afternoon, not feeling like attacking the bungalow that day.

We started early the following day, with Heather's fiancé Kevin leading the way with disposal of rubbish. I worried something vital might end up on his bonfire, but he assured me he was checking everything and I had to agree there were a great number of boxes and papers that had only one destination. Heather was not quite as enthusiastic, firstly looking in horror at the dark rooms, demanding plastic gloves before she started on anything. While the rest of us were scrabbling through blackened rubbish, she very gingerly picked up the odd ornament or glass and popped it into a cardboard box.

Once Aub, Mark and Kevin had removed the boards from the windows we were able to see Ken's wonderful model railway collection in the hall, sadly, partly melted by the heat. I was relieved he'd already given me the models my grandfather had handmade, it was sad to see the damage, but would have been far worse if they had been there.

Gradually, we started to make inroads through the bungalow. There was a toilet in one of the bedrooms, not walled off, just fitted and in working order (or had been) in the corner of the room. This and the other dark pink bathroom fittings were now black.

While the men continued to feed the huge bonfire, crackling away in the large garden, Heather and I worked on the sitting room. This had been the least affected by the fire as the door had been shut, but was still fairly daunting. Books had taken over the entire room. Ken had ordered large, coffee-table type books from several book clubs, but not singly, at least two copies of most. He'd also bought shirts in sixes, and pairs of shoes in excess. I'm sure he'd been lonely and enjoyed the visits from the postman. This is probably why the postman found him, being a regular visitor.

"Isn't it time we had lunch?" Heather asked, fed up with the proceedings. She'd pulled faces every time she had to pick up something unidentifiable and Aub's warning to look out for rats hadn't improved the situation.

"Yes, let's find a pub," I said. "Give the others a shout, I'll get the wet wipes"

After a cold hand wash under the outside tap, Heather and I chose wet wipes for our faces. The men just looked a bit black. Having checked on the bonfire, we drove to Cenarth to find a decent pub. There were two and sadly, we probably picked the slightly more 'spit and sawdust' one. Heather took off to the ladies to clean up again, while I looked at the menu ordered. When I joined her, she was horrified.

"It's disgusting in there. We might catch something."

The toilets were quite clean really, but it was all too much for her, after the rats and squalor of Ken's burnt out house. After lunch, Kevin decided it was a good time to return home with Heather, as her enthusiasm was definitely waning.

Before we returned to the hotel that evening, Aub and Mark decided to put another pile of rubbish on the now dead bonfire, but not light it until the following day. They didn't want any dramas. When we arrived the following morning, the entire rubbish pile was burnt. It turned out that the long dead bonfire had only been sleeping and when the wind got up the flames were licked into action. John, the neighbouring farmer, thought the bungalow had caught fire again during the night, as he could see flames billowing out. A good thing it was well down the garden.

Eventually the book problem was partially solved. We selected a few to keep, returned those that hadn't even been unwrapped (again often in pairs), then contacted a book shop in Hay on Wye who sent a man with a large van. After a full day of sifting through those of interest to him, he loaded up over 1000 books and paid us just over £1200. This left us with just a few hundred to box up for Oxfam. Perhaps they should all have gone there, but the challenge of delivering them was more than we could face. The excess shirts were passed around the family and offered to John the farmer next door.

Our next move was for a tree surgeon to remove the two lines of huge Leylandii that were blocking out all the light. We feared those closest to the bungalow were interfering with the drainage pipes. I found him through yellow pages (and a wonderful job he did) then John found another man to haul out the roots. The area looked totally different.

Once probate was sorted, we needed estimates for renovating the property. Having never dreamed of inheriting the bungalow, we couldn't bring ourselves to sell it, or certainly not in its present state. When the large local building firm sent an astronomical bill for boarding up the windows, we decided to look elsewhere. Just by chance, we asked the tree surgeon, who was local, if he knew of anyone.

"Barry's a good chap, just redone our kitchen. I don't know if he'd take this on."

Barry agreed to come and look and it was the best move we could have made. A very sincere and honest man, he managed the whole refurbishment for us and we couldn't have been happier.

At this time, alongside farming, I was helping Mark out with the admin part of his new business, something I said I'd do for the first six months and ended up there for the next six years! Several weeks after Ken's funeral, Mark came bouncing up the stairs in his new premises in Gloucester, tossing a large, obviously light, cardboard box in the air.

"Something arrived for you, mother. What've you been sending for?"

"That's your uncle," I said, looking at the details. Mark looked horrified. "Oh, don't worry; Ken would have seen the funny side of you throwing him up the stairs."

As we hadn't stayed in Wales long enough to collect Ken's ashes, the undertakers had posted them.

On rereading his letters there had been, well, more of a desire than a request, that his ashes were scattered in Ravello, in Northern Italy, where his heart must always have been.

Only months before his death, he'd written about a dream: a golden light streaming through an opening door then the silhouette of a woman leaving through this door. He was convinced this was a signal his Italian love had died. Being equally sure she would still have lived near Ravello, he wished to be reunited with her. If nothing else, I felt we owed him this.

I had no reason to believe that Ken's marriage to Ivy had been unhappy, although I gathered from his later letters that it sounded pretty mundane. The young uncle I remember from my childhood had always been a smart dresser. While dapper may be the wrong word, David Suchet's interpretation of Poirot is always reminiscent of the younger Ken.

He and Ivy had ballroom-danced together to a high level. Once they gave up dancing, I fear they had discovered they had very little else in common. He was such a great uncle when I was small and would have made a good father, but they had no children, whether from choice I don't know. He loved walking and climbing, something Ivy never shared, but they stayed together for life. His letters told me that his heart longed to return elsewhere.

"A week on the Amalfi coast incorporates a day in Ravello," I told Aubrey, showing him the holiday guide.

"Sounds good to me. Mind you, if Ken had wanted his ashes scattered in Birmingham, I'd have sent you on your own, but I'd better come with you to Ravello!"

After considerable research about taking the ashes through customs, we were slightly taken aback when the airline representative didn't require any proof of the content of the box, simply tossing them through the baggage area, similar to their arrival at the Mark's office.

This was in late October, a suitable time for a holiday. Hopefully the ewes were all in lamb, most meat lambs sold and other young stock happy in the fields, so it was fairly easy to leave the farm for a while. The hotel I'd booked was fine, if not exciting. The room comfortable and meals just a little above school dinner grade, but we managed to lunch out at wonderful fish restaurants and met up with some lovely people.

The weather excelled itself. The sea was turquoise and calm and the sun deliciously warm, without being too hot. I'd booked several coach trips which took us to all the wonders of the Amalfi coast including Ravello at the end of our week. Clutching the casket, Aub had to explain its contents to another passenger who worried we were carrying a bomb.

Ravello is beautiful. Pictures of the village, with its umbrella pines, perched high above the Mediterranean, are often used in advertisements. We walked up the hill from the coach, bougainvillea spilling from every window box, draping brilliant reds and purples along the white washed walls. What a wonderful place to lay Ken to rest. Finding somewhere not crawling with late summer tourists was the problem.

"Let's go up here," Aub said, pointing to some shallow stone steps, doubling away from the main hub of the village. At the top, a little way along a lane, we found a small private garden, obviously connected to one of the expensive hotels either side, and overlooking the azure sea. The small grass area, with beds of Busy Lizzy, looked ideal, but hotel guests were wandering around. Once they left, I carried the casket of ashes into the garden while Aub stood guard, menacingly, at the gate.

"Don't be long," he warned. "There are more people coming."

Luckily, he had already taken the top off the casket for me, so saying a few words, expressing my hopes that he'd met up with his lady and thanking him for leaving us the bungalow, I scattered Ken's remains over the Busy Lizzies. The breeze would soon remove any left on the flowers rather than the soil. I'd love to have scattered his ashes over the cliff onto the coast, but with the strong breeze I could have been wearing them.

"Come on," Aub hissed.

I left the garden as a further group of people arrived at the gate. We wandered back to the village centre, where Aub, without ceremony, stuffed the casket into a rubbish bin.

Another thank you to Ken was this delightful week in sunny Italy, to a place we may never have visited had we not fulfilled his wishes.

Ken, who loved the great outdoors

CHAPTER 37

German Export

Last autumn we had the farmyard newly concreted. This was fantastic, although it did make life a little awkward moving sheep around while work was in progress.

Fortunately, and with no advance notification, machinery arrived the day after we'd put a selection of rams with synchronised ewes, occupying every stable and shed we have in the yard. Had the builders made the decision to start a day earlier, life would have been utter chaos.

Into our second week of limited access to the main yard, we were coping quite well. We did need a bulk feed delivery, but the lorry wouldn't have access to blow the feed in. Luckily, we were feeding so few we could operate out of tote bags in the grain store, which was not affected by the builders. We were also utilising this area to secure and load the last of the rams to go, persuading them to pass the main yard gateway when they came in from the field, where their feet would have done little to improve the concrete. These rams had been sold earlier and were now departing to different areas of the UK ... and Germany.

Exports can either be the icing on the cake or a complete and utter headache. So much effort goes into showing these sheep to our customers, and accepting all their requirements, that it's usually a day of great relief when we see the animals leave.

On this occasion the ram bound for Germany didn't give us any problems, other than losing his Electronic ID tag. A replacement had been duly ordered, along with a spare visual tag, because you never know, sheep are quite capable of losing all identification at the last moment. As this chap had been blood tested for Brucella Ovis, and his full travel log filled in, the loss of a tag at the last minute would be disaster.

2514 was due to be vetted and all forms completed around 10am on the Thursday, with Theo, the transporter, collecting him around midday. Then the evening before his departure I had a message from Theo: he would like to collect the sheep at 7:30am and could we arrange for the vet to come earlier?

Now, Graham is very helpful on these occasions, but I felt expecting him to come at 6:30am was really not on. However, he agreed to 7:30am as traffic should be good then, as he had to cross Gloucester. Theo could come after 8:30 am, as the paperwork would take around an hour to complete.

An early start for everyone. Before the yard was filled with builder's vehicles, we moved 2514 and his companion from the main sheep shed to a freshly bedded small pen in the grain store. It would be easy for Graham to check him over here and to see him move without chasing him round the yard. I then collected the pliers from the office for Aub to put in the tag before Graham arrived.

"Hang on," I said. "I'll get a rope to hold him with."

"He'll be fine. Just put a hand under his chin."

Oh, his confidence in my ability. 2514 was a fair specimen of eighteen month old Texel sheep. I should have insisted, I wasn't sure I could hold him without a rope round his neck, but hindsight is always good. I climbed into the pen, put a hand under his chin and held as tight as I could.

As Aub replaced the tag in the original hole, therefore not causing any pain or discomfort, the ram leapt forward and half the yellow EID tag flew out of the pliers, into the bright yellow straw, never to be seen again. Well, we certainly struggled to see it. After grovelling in the straw on our hands and knees, then lifting half the area and shaking out each forkful so the tag should fall on the concrete, Graham drove into the yard.

"This the boy then?" he asked.

"Yes, but we've just lost his EID tag in the straw," I said.

Aub was still grovelling round on his hands and knees.

"Let's have a look at him," Graham said, able to check that his identity matched the paperwork from the visual tag. He examined the ram to see he looked healthy and moved well. "Haven't you got a reader? You'd find it quicker."

No, we don't have an electronic reader. One would be very useful, particularly this morning, but they are quite costly and so far we've not seen the need for one.

I remembered Aub's cousins a few miles away had one. "If Graham and I do the paperwork you could borrow that. Couldn't you?"

Aub muttered in agreement, still furious that I hadn't held the ram still. We both realised that after all the planning, blood tests etc. 2514 wasn't going anywhere without his correct EID tag. We had to find it. It was too early for the village children to be at the school, but I had thought of bribing them to come and search through the straw.

Back to the house with Graham, having made us cups of tea, we went through the export paperwork as painstakingly as always. The journey log was checked; the ram had been born on the farm and never been off, so his health status wasn't in any way compromised; his blood test results were clear. I photocopied all the completed paperwork, with its overlapping stamps on every page, one copy for us, the other to travel with the ram. All in all this took the expected hour, and still no sign of Aub to say he'd found the tag. Although, thinking about it, he may have been doing something else up at the farm, waiting for us to return. He wouldn't be re-tagging him on his own.

When Graham and I arrived, Aub was pulling out what remains of his hair.

"Martin's reader's next to useless. When I got it here it wouldn't work at all. I took it back to change the batteries, then the bloody thing acknowledges the tag from such a distance I still can't see it, and it's not one of those readers that will repeat the signal."

"Well, let's all have a look," Graham suggested. "More eyes must be helpful. I'm really sorry, if we can't find it I'll have to send this paperwork back to Carlisle and he won't be able to go."

Suddenly, moving the straw again at the back of the pen, I saw one half of the tag.

"I've found half of it," I shouted, "but not both bits."

"The other bit's still in the pliers. How on earth did you find that with your eyesight?"

There was really no answer for that, but with great relief and a thick rope to hold him, I managed to pin the ram to the side of the hurdle while Aub, successfully this time, attached the tag in his ear. Graham left grinning. Then all we had to do was wait for the transport, expected any minute. Theo arrived at midday.

Transport times and arrangements for exports can be the proverbial nightmare, travel logistics causing disruption.

Six years ago we had interest from a Belgian farm, wishing to take six breeding ram lambs. On this occasion their office was doing all their own paperwork and providing transport, as the lorry had dairy heifers coming into the UK. All looked good until the driver rang me late in the day to say he'd been held up and wouldn't have time to reach our farm and catch the ferry he'd booked. Could we meet him on his way down from Shropshire?

This was how we came to be parked in an unlit lay-by at midnight, waiting for a Belgian lorry to collect the ram lambs we had on board. I'd suggested we met at a local pub car park not far from his suggested lay-by, but the driver was horrified at the thought. He didn't want to meet anywhere where there were lights or someone might see us! Wondering if we were being too trusting, I began to doubt he'd come.

"He sounded genuine and they've paid for the lambs," said Aub. "I expect he will."

Eventually a huge lorry, looking like a giant Christmas decoration pulled up behind us. The young driver apologised profusely for the change in arrangements, explaining he had been delayed unloading the heifers earlier. He introduced himself.

"Hi," he said. "I'm Bum."

"Bum?" I said. "You can't be called Bum!"

He laughed. He had a thatch of blond hair and sparkling blue eyes, and had obviously had this reaction to his name before.

"It doesn't mean the same in my country as it does in yours."

We all laughed and agreed that it couldn't. Whatever his name, he seemed very well organised and his lorry was immaculate; deep bedded with clean straw, automatic water and a rack full of lovely meadow hay.

We sorted through the paperwork, as Bum emphasised, with export the paperwork is far more important to the authorities than the animals. Then we backed the trailer up to the open lorry ramp and the lambs wandered through with no problem. They seemed very content in their new surroundings and we were pleased to return home to bed. Although situations can be a little unorthodox at times, we do meet the nicest of people involved with livestock.

The lambs were soon on their way to the ferry and we received confirmation of their safe arrival later that day.

It can be just as chaotic when we deliver our rams in person. I had some rams that needed delivering to UK customers who didn't own livestock trailers. It's often a good day out, and on this occasion when I needed to deliver two rams to a farmer near Hungerford, my great friend Sharon decided to keep me company and navigate.

It was a beautiful sunny October morning. We set off, laughing at my chance to escape the farm for a few hours. I'd obviously been too vague about lunch arrangements, as Sharon came prepared with a delicious picnic.

"We don't get out together very often, so let's make a fun day of it," she said, settling herself in the passenger seat with the map and the address.

We were to deliver a ram lamb en route, to a farm I'd never been to before, so I'd jotted down the instructions the farmer's wife had given me over the phone. I passed these to my 'navigator' – it was just unfortunate she couldn't read my writing!

"Winplot," she said, loudly. "We're looking for a place called Winplot."

I glanced over at my notes. "Wroughton," I corrected. "It's Wroughton. If you see Winplot on any of the signposts we'll go there."

We took the signs to Wroughton.

"Beds farm on left, what's that?" she asked a little later.

"No idea," I said, so when it was possible, I pulled over to glance at my notes. "After bends, farm on left, stupid."

Sharon raised her eyebrows then tried to ignore me.

"Biplane on lights." This was Sharon's final offering.

By now I was shaking with laughter. "What are you talking about?"

"That's what it says, Biplane on lights."

The penny dropped. "Oh, bungalow on right, yes, I think this is where we turn off."

Amazingly we'd arrived at the right place. The ram lamb was unloaded and admired, then duly presented to his women, although he immediately formed a desire to stay with a wether (castrated ram) lamb, rather than join the main flock.

"I suppose we've got a dumbo here," sighed his new owner, as her husband and I tried to persuade the ram lamb that females were more interesting.

"You wanted a big one with good back end, you didn't mention intelligence as a factor," I shouted back to her, laughing. Fairly soon the lamb was getting the idea and the ewes were jolly keen to see him. After collecting a cheque and retrieving Sharon from the calf pens, going gooey eyed over the babies, we set off for Hungerford.

With Sharon in charge we left the M4 at Junction 15. I drove round the large motorway roundabout enquiring which exit Sharon fancied.

"I think its Marlborough, we don't want to go back to Cirencester, do we?"

"We don`t want to go to Marlborough either." I passed that exit and continued on round, much to the consternation of other drivers. I was probably in the wrong lane but kept indicating where I thought we should be going, hoping no one would drive into me.

"Look, there are only three exits, it can't take rocket

science," I grumbled.

Sharon rifled in the back for the map book. "Well I can see Hungerford but I can't see Marlborough."

"It's a very large-scale map. Can you make a decision before I do a fourth circuit and the police arrive? They'll think I'm demonstrating or something?"

"We want the M4 to London," Sharon was very definite. "Junction 14 not 15."

Conveniently, we were just approaching that exit for the fifth time. Back on the M4, I glanced at the fuel gauge, we'd soon need petrol.

"Don't get it on the motorway, far more expensive," Sharon assured me, so we decided to get it on the way back. A bad move.

All was fairly uneventful until we reached the farm, delivered the rams and after coffee with the farmer and his wife in a very cosy country kitchen, returned to the car. I turned the key. Nothing happened. Dead as a door nail, it wouldn't even turn over.

The RAC were summoned. Although it would be a good hour's wait, we declined the kind offer of the farmer's kitchen and elected to sit in the car, consume Sharon's beautiful picnic and chat about life. Here we were in beautiful countryside, with the sun warming the inside of the car, delightfully comfortable. All would be well when the RAC man arrived.

Eventually, a very pleasant young man appeared who looked about fourteen. With Sharon's unrivalled assistance, he diagnosed a problem with either the starter or the battery, which I'd thought fairly obvious. I pointed out that he really ought to make his own decisions and not listen to Sharon as her directions and reading of pace notes left a lot to be desired. Personally, I didn`t think her knowledge of mechanics was much better.

To my amazement, Sharon suddenly turned from a sensible, middle-aged mother of two, both probably older than our charming RAC boy, into the sort of woman who could toss her long auburn hair. She leant over the engine as he looked under the bonnet.

"Sharon," I hissed, hoping he couldn't hear, as he sat back in the driver's seat and tried to start the car again. "Give it a rest. You'll frighten the poor boy out of his wits."

Actually, he was giving her sunny face a returning smile, or maybe it was her well-endowed chest making itself very obvious as she leant over the engine with him.

"I think it's probably the battery," he assured me and Sharon promptly agreed. Jump leads were produced and the car roared into life.

Thanking our rescuer profusely, and scowling at Sharon to behave, I drove off with his warning 'not to stop the car for any reason' still ringing in my ears.

Sharon reminded me that we needed petrol. As we reached the main road, I slammed on the brakes, manoeuvred the trailer across the farm drive so our escort could not escape, leapt out and accosted the poor man. He winced visibly, pointing out he had two other breakdowns waiting. Undaunted, I assured him I was his priority and was not letting him go until he'd finished with our breakdown. I couldn't fill the car with the engine running and he couldn't restart the car with jump leads on a garage forecourt.

"OK," he said, wearily. Obviously, even Sharon paled into insignificance when he calculated his timescale and other waiting motorists. "There's a garage not far from here. Follow me; I'll indicate where you can park nearby. I'll fill the fuel can, fill your car then jump start it again. I'll just have to call in and explain that I've been held up for longer than expected."

I moved my car and trailer out of his way, and we followed him to a small village.

All worked to plan. I paid the eight pounds odd for the petrol, which should just get us home and, again, thanked him profusely for his help.

"Eight pounds!" he said. "I can remember when £5 would have filled that."

"Can you really?" I was surprised because that would have been some time ago, which meant he was much older than I'd thought. Getting back in the car I realised how stupid I'd been.

I turned to Sharon, "He just said he could remember when we could have filled up for a fiver. I was really impressed; I thought he meant the car, he meant the petrol can!"

Our valiant RAC man suggested we drove home via the B roads as a call-out on the motorway could be tricky. We followed his instructions, having a good giggle.

"You were appalling, flirting with that poor young man," I accused Sharon

"I was not flirting," she said indignantly. "He just fancied me."

Nearing home, we stopped at a pub for a restorative glass

of wine, and agreed to keep our day to ourselves. It came as a bit of a shock to realise how many years must have passed since we'd first made a delivery run like this.

CHAPTER 38

A horse called Goose

I suppose Goose was a sort of rescue. A beautiful rocking horse dapple grey mare, bred in the pink for eventing, she'd been sold by her breeder, but failed the vetting having been found to be a head shaker. Due to be put down, I was offered her as a brood mare – the condition was not known to be hereditary.

In retrospect, I paid more than meat price for her, but she was lovely. Her full title was The Baroness, born the day Margaret Thatcher became Prime Minister, but being grey, with a long neck, she'd earned herself the nickname Goose, far preferable.

Cecil, who did a lot of transport jobs for us at the time, delivered her with dire warnings about her behaviour, making me wonder if the purchase had been wise. But never once did she give me any doubts about her behaviour, she was the sweetest of horses and much loved. As with most of our mares at that time, she was put in foal to Masterpiece. I'm not sure what colour I was anticipating for the foal with a cross between grey and skewbald, but the very solid, definite dark brown of

Miserden Velvet was unexpected.

Velvet was born late one night. Goose had been out with some other mares and I feel I was perhaps a little late separating her, which may have added to her problems. Once brought into the foaling box it was only a few hours before she gave birth, but something was wrong. We had cameras in the stable, and once I saw she was getting down to foal, I drove up to the yard. The foal had a leg turned back at the knee. A frantic call to Aub and between us and Goose the birth was successful, the foal up and sucking within a short time. I left her to cleanse and sort herself out, keeping an eye on the camera and popping back to the yard a little later. It was then I discovered she'd prolapsed slightly.

This really showed my lack of experience with horses' foaling. Ewes can prolapse and we simply push it back in, give antibiotics and anti-inflammatory injections and all is fine. Compared to a sheep, this was small, about the size of a tennis ball. To be on the safe side I rang the emergency vet, who came out around 6am and dealt with the problem. She continued to come for the next three days, washing Goose out and checking all was good. On day three, after she'd left saying all should be fine, we put Goose and her foal in a paddock by the buildings and thought all was well. It was only a few hours later I realised Goose was walking strangely. She had laminitis.

Toxic laminitis, which occurs after foaling, is devastating. It took us a long time to persuade Goose she could walk up the field and back into her stable. Sadly, she never left it again.

Knowing what I know now, I'd have done my best to find a surrogate mother for the foal and had Goose put down far earlier. But with constant veterinary advice and treatment and an excellent blacksmith we made her life bearable. The mare loved her child and reared her for two months. At this point the foal could now continue on milk pellets and I couldn't keep poor Goose any longer. Even as Aub led her out to be put down, her crippled feet nerve-blocked to mask the pain, the vet was trying to assure me there were further things he could do for her, but I knew she was suffering and couldn't put her through more.

We've lost sheep though lambing problems and it's upsetting, but nothing compares to losing a horse. Goose was such a sweet mare. She may have come with health warnings, but I adored her. Although the reasons for her laminitis are scientifically unknown, I felt the awful guilt of having let her down and cried unending tears for her. All I could promise her was that we would look after her foal.

Ella, Mark's long retired miniature Shetland pony became Miserden Velvet's substitute mother. A little unsure of the situation, as this foal was far bigger than her, Ella stood her ground in the stable, turning into a small mechanical beast that could bite, kick and buck if this foal annoyed her. I didn't know whether to laugh or cry. Poor Velvet was distressed at losing her mother and Ella was slightly un-nerved, but they spent the next four years devoted to each other.

Velvet was fed on milk pellets four times a day, with her manger high off the ground so Ella couldn't reach. Initially at feed times the mechanical savage little horse returned, but Ella was soon satisfied with a small helping of sugar beet pulp and mash at the same time. Within days they were out in the paddock, something completely new to Velvet, who probably couldn't remember her first few hours outside. She would canter round Ella in small circles, bucking and leaping, whinnying in ecstasy, while Ella stood her ground watching. A manger was tied on the top rail of the fence and Ella still had her four small feeds a day on the ground and blossomed.

When I started lunging and long-reining Velvet, before she went away to be backed as a four-year-old, Ella's interest was very obvious. By this time Velvet was happily living with other youngsters on the farm, but whenever I took her along to the paddock to be lunged, Ella would appear to see how she was progressing. It was very special to see Ella watching her progeny. She always seemed to know, even if she was on the far side of the farm, and would appear from nowhere.

Velvet turned into a beautiful young horse and became another success story. Ellie, a talented young rider, was looking for a potential event horse and Miserden Velvet (to give her full name) ticked all the boxes. She did blot her copy book when Ellie rode her out the first time, bucking her off, but nothing dissuaded Ellie that she was the right horse for her and she and Velvet had an excellent eventing career. Being fairly local meant I could watch at some of the events, which was great.

The pair competed up to Novice eventing CIC*, anticipating their move to Intermediate, then unfortunately Velvet sustained an injury to a hind suspensory ligament in 2012. Well on the way to recovery she injured herself again, so in 2013 she was given a holiday and put in foal to show jumper Cevin Z. The following year, Velvet produced a beautiful filly foal. Calling her Callista, Ellie asked if she could add Miserden to the name, so now we look forward to what appears to be a very talented grey mare, Miserden Callista, following in her mother's footsteps.

These days, Velvet is back in light work and obviously has a home for life. I'm sure Goose would be delighted.

Ella became Velvet's devoted substitute mother

Our grandchildren spend a lot of
time with the animals on the farm

CHAPTER 39

Spot, Dot and Christmas

Christmas on the farm begins as it does for many people, I should imagine. From mid-November, strains of *Once in Royal David's City* waft through the open windows of the village school. At certain times of the day a crocodile of excited small children are shepherded to the nearby village hall for secret rehearsals of *The Wizard of Oz* or *Aladdin*, or, these days, something more modern.

We're lucky to have grandchildren at different schools, so we get to do the Christmas play twice.

Heather and Kevin's son Leo was First Voiceover in a combination of *Strictly* and *X Factor*, where the judges were an inn keeper's wife, a donkey and a Caesar reminiscent of Craig Revel Horwood. Mark and Kate's son Wilfred was in a play that took four children around the world to see Christmas in different places. Both plays fared better than some we've heard of. Last year a friend's little girl was a frog called Mary and she and Joseph went to Spiderman's house in a minibus, along with five Elsa's from *Frozen*. The meaning of that nativity play was somehow lost in translation!

When our children were at Miserden School, I remember looking through the school windows at all the decorations and paperchains we'd heard so much about over the preceding weeks. These eventually arrived home and I have to admit I was always a sucker for anything our children had diligently produced. Only a few years ago, when well into her thirties, Heather did suggest I binned the large red star she'd made at primary school. She felt it made our rather smart Christmas decorations look tatty.

"Are you sure?" I asked. "You were so proud of it when you brought it home."

"Mum, I was six. I hope both my taste and my artistic skills have improved slightly since then. But I do love you for keeping it."

Since then, several rather moth-eaten projects have been surreptitiously discarded. Now I welcome our grandchildren's Christmas decorations with as much delight as I did our children's.

The last day of term was still to come. A morning carol service, well practiced by very vocal children and illustrated by Mary, Joseph, the donkey and plenty of adoring shepherds and angels, along with carrot monsters, stone-aged men and the occasional octopus.

Once school has finished, home, family and adventures are the focal point, with the lead-up to the big day. In recent years Aub has taken our grandsons on a Christmas tree hunt, to cut one down and drag it home, as shown in American films. He did actually find a lady who wanted a number of trees removing from the back of her field. This fitted the bill perfectly. A daring mission under the cover of near darkness, the boys convinced we were doing it quietly and secretly. Another exciting adventure with Grandpa.

There always seems to be some drama with livestock around the Christmas period, but neither of us expected this to involve Mark's Gloucester Old Spot pigs. Spot and Dot were well established at what we loosely termed 'the satellite farm' – so called because although they were Mark's animals we'd somehow become responsible for making a detour to feed said pigs, after we'd checked and fed all our sheep.

Mark had purchased Bisley Lane Farm, and his first venture was to rear two young sows he could handle well and would become pets for his children. Then they could produce offspring for 'Spot and Dot Charcuterie'.

Initially, Spot and Dot lived in one of our stables at Sudgrove, but as they grew, and started to greet us over the door most mornings, it seemed time that they had their own, purpose-built quarters on Mark's farm.

They now resided in a quarter of an acre of pine wood, fenced by sheep netting with a circuit of electric fence running around the base of the enclosure, to prevent them from digging their way out. While this was a far better solution in the first instance than our restrictive stable, as the winter's weather deteriorated their conditions weren't ideal. Constant rain and Spot and Dot's persistent industrial resurfacing of their pen had left the ground waterlogged and I felt they must be fed up with wandering round in thick cold mud all day.

Typically, I was shouted down as 'I knew nothing about pigs' – which I had to agree with. The trouble was that I wasn't sure how much Mark and Aubrey knew either. I was assured as long as they had a warm, deeply strawed ark where they could snuggle up together, pigs enjoyed being out in mud. This proved not to be the case.

On the morning of 23rd December, we were only greeted by one anxious, hungry pig. Dot was nowhere to be seen. She eventually emerged from the ark, hunched up and stiff. Definitely not a happy girl. She did come in to feed, but without her usual enthusiasm, and two very worried pig-carers drove home to ring the vet. At this point the pig owner was in Cornwall with Kate and the children for Christmas week with his in-laws. It was down to us to deal with the matter.

First finding a vet to discuss the problem with was not totally straightforward. As they were Mark's pigs, I rang the Cirencester vets, where I knew he took his dog. They had no intention of dealing with a pig. No worries, I rang our farm vets and Graham, as helpful as always, discussed the situation. Were they vaccinated against erysipelas? Probably not, I surmised. Well they should be and if that was what we were treating they needed pen and strep for three days and an anti-inflammatory drug. If it looked like pneumonia, which we decided it did, then five days. Best to inject just below the ear, between the ear and the shoulder.

"Great. We've got to catch her first," was Aub's response.

Armed with syringes and antibiotics we drove back to the pig's wood, where Spot paraded for us, thankfully showing she was fit and well, while Dot hid in the ark. Aub thrust the syringes at me and told me to bang on the back of the ark.

"She might come out."

Or she might not. Eventually he resorted to clambering in with Dot and manoeuvring her round until he was able to push her outside. Breathing heavily and red in the face he shouted instructions as to where I should stand to help catch her. Dot had no intention of coming anywhere near us, even if she did feel rough.

"Don't let her get back in the bloody house again," he yelled as I failed to extricate my feet from the mud quickly enough, and she took to her bed again. After another period of Aub snuggling up to her in the ark, and a great deal of vocal discussion from them both, Dot and Aub appeared once more.

"Just stand in front of the ark, you're pretty useless at helping catch her. Just stop her going back to bed."

I did as I was told. No point trying to explain I was struggling to stay upright, let alone wade quickly enough through glue and a small forest. After a couple more circuits I offered a suggestion.

"Can't you lasso her and tie her to a tree?"

Scathing probably describes the expression on my husband's face, but within five minutes he'd gone in search of rope. Sidling alongside Dot, who had now ceased galloping around the pen, he managed to slip a noose round her neck and secure it to a tree. She pulled back and squealed for all she was worth then plunged forward like a crocodile in a death roll.

"Quick, give me the stuff."

I'd already approached with the syringes, but Aub only managed to inject one drug before he panicked, thinking she was going to kill herself. The noise was unreal; her facial expressions showed no amusement. Relaxing the rope and pressure on her neck, the livid pig became a little more user-friendly, and though the burns on Aub's hands didn't improve his mood, he was finally able to administer the second antibiotic. Gradually he released her from the noose and she took to her bed again.

Covered by antibiotics and in the warm was the best we could do at that moment. We'd try to get help tomorrow morning (Christmas Eve!), to guide them into the small trailer so that we could take them home with us. We'd already attempted this, having reversed the trailer into the gateway and removed the strand of electric fence, but neither Dot nor Spot would cross the line where it had been. It had definitely been a severe deterrent against escape and its ghost was still there! Aub wasn't keen to leave the gate open allowing access to the trailer in case we lost them altogether so we decided to wait.

The next day, on Christmas Eve, it was with great relief that we were greeted by two fairly healthy-looking pigs in the morning, although Spot was still keener on breakfast than Dot.

In fairness to Mark, he had offered to drive back, but then decided he could call on his local friends to help. Our assistants were Jono and Hugo from Edgeworth, and Martin, who'd only dropped by with a bottle of whisky (for allowing him to shoot over our ground), and foolishly offered to help.

They all stood round with the boards Aub had found. The intention was to drive the pigs up the now accessible trailer ramp, which still meant crossing the 'ghost' electric fence line. Spot had no intention of doing this. While I was tempting her with pig nuts and Hugo and Jono herding from behind, Dot was trying to seek refuge in her house. By this time, Martin, who'd been issued with a board that needed two men to carry it, was so deeply bogged down in mud he'd lost all ability to move. Aub leapt at Dot, doing all he could to deter her from reaching the ark, when she stopped suddenly and he found himself astride her. As they took off between the trees the entertainment was too good for the rest of us to waste time with Spot. Finally, Jono and Hugo went to Aub's assistance, and while he dragged himself from the mud, they herded Dot towards the gate. Martin was glued to the spot and likely to need assistance to extricate himself. Somehow, we trapped Dot between a hurdle and the gate so Aub could get in with her to administer the morning's antibiotics. Once he had her in an enclosed area and stroked her hairy neck, she accepted her injection with good grace. A relief to everyone.

"Thank you so much gentlemen for all your help," said Aub, once everyone had pulled themselves from the quagmire.

We decided to leave the trailer there with the gates secured round it and hope they'd wander in overnight and we could catch them in the morning. Later we heard when Mark rang to thank his friends, Jono said it had been worthwhile just to see Aub riding a pig through the woods!

Aub and I agreed we would probably manage without

assistants the following morning. It would be Christmas Day after all, and they all had young families. We put the feed trough, with some pig nuts in the trailer and then it was just a waiting game.

Christmas morning was similar to any other, with the routine of feeding and checking livestock, but for once the weather was kind. By the time we reached our satellite farm the sun was shining and both sows greeted us with excitement at the sight of their breakfast. Aub crept round to man the ramp gate as I put pig nuts, appetising apples and vegetable peelings into their trough in the trailer. Spot and Dot walked happily straight into the trailer to their feast. Aub shut the gates and the ramp. It had been so easy.

Soon both girls were established in a warm, freshly strawed stable, now their winter quarters, certainly until their wooded hideout had dried out a little. Dot stood quietly for the next two days with no sign of worry or resentment while Aub injected her each morning.

Mark hadn't exactly been flavour of the day initially, but we had to admit that his pigs were very well-handled and this did make them extremely nice to care for ... once we'd secured them.

We drove back to the house, breathing a huge sigh of relief. The sheep were fed and upright and Dot was well on the road to recovery. It was time for a shower, then lunch with Heather, Kev and Leo, and finally we might get the chance to enjoy a 'normal' Christmas afternoon.

CHAPTER 40

Showing and Judging

If Christmas is about family, then summer for a sheep farmer is about livestock shows. The summer showing season is great fun. Not just the competition, although that is important, but meeting up with friends from different parts of the country that we haven't seen for months, especially after a long winter and hard lambing. Sometimes our summer is so busy that we barely stop.

In 2019, having hoped for a warm, dry Three Counties, we were left with a cold, grey one – and if you think all farmers spend their time worrying about the weather, and rarely being satisfied with what they get, you'd be right! The trouble is, being outside all the time, it affects us so much.

The weather on Friday, judging day, was kind though and there was even a glimmer of sunshine while we were in the ring. With both Texels and Blue Texels being judged on the same day, we rarely get back to the marquee before prize winners are called for the Grand Parade late in the afternoon. We often make the decision that the sheep have been out in the rings long enough that day and it would be unfair to persuade them to come out again, especially as that time the older ones were not behaving very well on halters!

There are two more days with parades we can take part in. On this occasion it was definitely the right decision. Just as the sheep competitors stood in the centre of the main ring, listening to the commentary and watching additional Championships being awarded, the heavens opened. They could do nothing but stand in the full force of the weather, collars up, heads bowed. When they arrived back at the marquees, all those who had opted to stay behind handed out towels to dry both handlers and sheep.

The sun did eventually return, with a vengeance. We had two sweltering days at the Royal Welsh followed by two days away delivering rams to Northumberland, where the temperature even on top of the Pennines reached an amazing 37 degrees. In the car the air conditioning did a valiant job, and luckily we were able to keep moving, so air flowed readily around the trailer to keep the rams cool.

We spend a lot of our life travelling. While we now limit ourselves to showing at The Royal Three Counties at Malvern and later in the year at Moreton in the Marsh, we can find ourselves judging all over the country.

Last year I started in May with a beautiful day at Shropshire County show, then Bath and West where the weather was as cold as I can remember. Watching the Texel classes in the morning I was frozen, but pleased to have a hot lunch and somewhere warm to change into my 'judge's outfit' for the afternoon of Blue Texels, although I still retained a wax coat and hat! The quality of the animals was good too, which always makes judging so much easier.

A few weeks later we both judged at two Welsh shows on consecutive weekends – a marathon of walking up and down the lines. I do love judging but I was quietly relieved to see from the calendar that our final show, at the beginning of August, would just involve Aub judging Blue Texels – my role was simply that of Judge's wife, admiring from the sidelines.

Needless to say, it was not to be.

The day before the show the secretary rang in a panic. Her judge for the Any Other Breed class was unwell so could I stand in and judge that class? As I would be there anyway, of course I agreed.

Then she added, "Oh and before that, could you just judge the Young Handlers ...?"

That was a bit of a bombshell as it's the class no one really wants to take on. While the children are fun to judge, some offering the most classic answers to questions, the onlooking parents can be terrifying.

Divided into two sections, 12 and under and 12 – 16 yrs, the class for younger competitors can be a bit daunting, but there are not usually too many entries. At Honiton, however, I walked into the ring to see twenty-two assorted under twelves clutching their lambs. Some looked very professional, as often very young children from farming families have been showing their own or the family's stock from an early age. Others looked as though they were unlikely to stay in charge of their pet for very long. But how to judge?

The only advice Aub had given me was "don't shout at

them or make them cry." I'm still not sure why he thought I would.

I decided that as some were there to win and were quite capable, I would simply ask them to lead their lamb forward a couple of steps and stand it ready for a judge to examine. (Handling them is just to see if the child can present it correctly for a judge. The quality of the animal is not judged.)

Those in control did this well and I was soon able to form a shortlist. I asked each child about their lamb, the youngest I simply asked the name and others I queried how much of the show preparation they had done. One small boy led out his Coloured Ryland lamb and stood it beautifully. He then described all the breed characteristics, showing me the white markings on the lamb's face, and most of the breed's history. He assured me that he had prepared his lamb himself and volunteered the information that he had already shown her at several shows. It was difficult not to be impressed.

Further down the line a tiny boy who I took to be about four, was clutching a small, but strong Beltex lamb. He looked very worried when I suggested he led it forward, but with my help he stayed attached and told me his lamb's name was Bubbles.

Three smartly turned-out boys nearer twelve in age, from a local school which runs its own farm, were also showing Beltex lambs. Their pristine white coats bore the school's name and each wore a white shirt and red tie. All in turn offered me their hand to shake and said a very polite 'Good Morning'.

The first led his lamb forward with little enthusiasm and when I asked if he did much with the sheep, assured me he'd rather be doing things with the cattle. There really wasn't an answer to that. The other two seemed more inclined to handling sheep although all three announced this was the first time they had shown a lamb. With each in turn I showed them how to check the lamb was standing correctly and place one hand under the lamb's chin to show it off to its best advantage for the judge. Hopefully this would stand them in a better position the next time they showed them.

Several other children knew what they were doing and offered me considerable detail about their lamb, so with the little boy with the Coloured Ryland winning that class I was able to find second to fourth quite easily. The twelve to sixteen year olds were mostly very professional which made selecting a winner a little more difficult, but again, a small girl with a Texel knew a lot about the breed characteristics and stood her lamb correctly while I handled it. Luckily everyone received a rosette and a bag of sweets. Nobody cried and even the parents looked happy about my decisions.

Judging the 'Any Other Breed' class was a walk in the park after my first two classes!

Later, Aub found worthy winners in the Blue Texels and we met up with numerous friends around the sheep pens. The camaraderie and social side of sheep breeding and shows is second to none, and certainly not limited to our own breeds of sheep.

Friends joined us for a delicious lunch in the members tent, overlooking the main ring where the heavy horses were being judged followed by a trick riding display. In all it was just a wonderful country show, enhanced by my 'Any Other

Breed' Champion, a Rouge de L'Ouest winning the Interbreed Championship.

After so many judging invitations that year, we agreed to judge at just one show during 2020, Aub with Texels and me Blue Texels at Suffolk County Show. It goes without saying that the year hasn't gone as planned for anyone, let alone the large livestock shows, and we were sorry to miss this. Hopefully the shows will be reinstated in 2021 and the fun will start again.

Chapter 41

Weird Times

It seems strange to end a book which is all about the people who have coursed through my life with a story of isolation, but 2020 is like no other for everyone. For farmers, the comparison of this crisis to the last Foot and Mouth outbreak is shockingly similar. It seems unbelievable that F&M happened nineteen years ago – cut off from our friends and neighbours for weeks, wondering if our livelihoods would still be there at the end of it.

Of course, in some ways, we've had a lot of practice at self-isolating. We do it most of the time. During lambing we're either in isolation in the sheep shed or asleep in an armchair. The larder is always well stocked. The feed bins are full, the barn stacked high with hay and straw.

Village life has its unique qualities too. Our village shop has done a wonderful job, stocking up as fast as they can and offering delivery services to those who can't leave home.

One morning in March, I listened to someone well-known suggesting we kept up our daily exercise. Obviously, he wasn't speaking directly to farmers. My first job of the morning was pushing the wheelbarrow of feed buckets round to all those sheep still in at nights. There was usually a riot of baaing when they saw me arrive with what must appear to them to be the sweet trolley. Luckily, we had enough sheds to accommodate the ewes and lambs, but they are scattered around the two farm yards. By mid-March the weather had improved after the long, wet winter, but some fields were still so waterlogged it was impossible to keep young lambs out at night, just to sleep in puddles. The good bite of grass eaten by the February flock hadn't really come back as yet. I pulled apart seven or eight slices of hay from a big bale, for the racks, so the ewes could fill up before being turned out for the day. By this point I felt as though I'd done my stint in the gym, and that was before I started to turn sheep out.

Aub had filled four bags of feed for the young rams and ewes at Edgeworth and driven off to struggle through the mud, fending off hungry sheep while he distributed feed along their troughs. I didn't envy him. Often having to empty the previous night's rainfall out of the troughs first, with about fifty wet, woolly bodies helping, it's not a great job.

In the main yard I opened the sheep shed gates, having alerted all ewes and lambs that it was time to venture out through the mud, to their daytime activity of finding grass. As the first field behind the barn was by now bare, they had to journey through to Top Verandas. At this point two ewes took off like greyhounds, with just one lamb each in tow. The second of their lambs wandered along aimlessly at the back of the queue. All were trying to take the small piece of high ground, to avoid the mud left by the tractor when they were being fed outside.

This would have worked quite well if the ewes at the back had been sensible and just kept on walking; but no, there is always one stupidly possessive mother who can't stand anyone other than her own child near her. Had the daft ewe with two orange spots on her back managed to keep going along the track with her child, also bearing two fluorescent orange spots, the two misplaced lambs would simply have followed and I could have mothered them up on arrival at Top Verandas. But no, Two Orange Spots decided these two harmless, lost little lambs were a definite threat to her only child and chased them away. They turned tail and returned to the yard.

Even with Maisie doing her level best to usher the lambs back to the field, I was fighting a losing battle. The dog and I followed the flock through the muddy track to the second field to gather up the entire flock of ewes and lambs. She made them retrace their steps back to the yard, where the two errant ewes suddenly remembered they were missing something. While I appreciated we were lucky not to be totally under water, as some Gloucester farms still were, the amount of rain we'd had meant the track left by the machinery was now a cross between liquid mud and glue. With great difficulty I managed to move, but with little alacrity, one foot stuck while the other performed abysmal ice dance movements through the flooded grass. Amazingly, with Maisie's help the lambs were re-united with their mothers, the entire flock reached the second field and I returned to the yard upright.

Which was more than Aub did. He returned spitting

blood, metaphorically, and covered in mud after some of the young rams decided he'd taken too long to fill the troughs. We still had two more lots to take to different fields, but decided we were well in front of the majority of the country on regular exercise.

I don't spend much time looking in the mirror. I probably should do more, when I notice the expressions on people's faces in the village shop. I must often look like I've been dragged through a hedge backwards. But no, the problem was different this time.

Our bathroom is small so I usually do catch sight of myself. It's just that day's reflection came as a surprise. After three weeks of dry sunny weather in April, that morning saw the arrival of drizzle and the promise of much needed rain – although after plodding around in the winter mud, I couldn't imagine ever using that phrase again. The misty drizzle was the problem. The reflection was that of a poodle, or at least a labradoodle.

A long time ago, when isolation wasn't the norm, Sharon said, "A light, soft perm would thicken your hair and just lift it a bit."

Sharon and I have been friends for many years. She's also my hairdresser. One of the joys of country-living is having a hairdresser three miles away, who is happy to be paid in lamb for the freezer and will fit me in at totally unreasonable times of the day or evening. My accountant is in the next village and is equally obliging. Although she does send me an annual bill, she's still available for queries at most times of the day.

That day, Sharon, who is an excellent hairdresser and really was convinced that a perm would improve my hairstyle, was now trying to work out why it went curly. "It's got to be your hair. The rollers I used are huge. No one else has come away with curly hair. Just keep combing it and it'll come straighter."

She was right of course. It did. But funnily enough when farming I rarely have a comb on me and certainly don't give a lot of thought to my hair. When she first did the perm, before lockdown, we went to supper at Heather and Kev's. My daughter looked me in the eye as I entered the kitchen. "Mother, can we discuss your hair?"

"Not much to discuss really," I said. It's a long time since I left a hairdresser and burst into tears because I didn't look anything like the magazine photo I'd taken with me. Or maybe it was the face under the hairstyle? But I'm too old to let these things worry me now.

"Just saying, but you look as though you've been electrocuted."

Since then we've been on lockdown and the only people I've seen are Aub and the sheep. The latter haven't commented, but one evening Aub asked me to comb my hair, as he couldn't hold a sensible conversation with a poodle.

23rd March 2020 was the first day of children being home from school. Suddenly relieved of the school-run, it made me smile when I heard people say they weren't sure whether to dress or simply stay in their nightwear.

It's a very long time since I began a day by going downstairs in my pyjamas and dressing-gown, but I remember the moment well. The fairly ancient dressing-gown was bright pink padded nylon, the accessories were pink floppy slippers. It was a Sunday morning. Aubrey had gone to work – we were then living at Pat Smythe's farm at Througham – but I'd lain in bed for a further hour, reading and dreaming, before deciding I'd like a cup of tea.

While filling the kettle I glanced out of the kitchen window to see Mule ewes wandering off along the road.

Dropping everything, I rushed out of the house after the escapees, eventually overtaking them and returning them to their field. Not before being passed by two cars and whistled at by our neighbour Richard while tripping over my floppy slippers. I vowed then never again to start the day in my nightclothes and haven't since. Jeans and trainers or wellies are much more suitable for our lifestyle.

Aub's and my journey from small holders in Througham to being full time farmers has been almost unbelievable. Had I taken the job with horses in Austria, none of this would have happened to me. Had I not come to Gloucestershire to work for Pat, I would never have met Aub. Life is full of ifs and buts.

While I have grown to love the sheep, some special ones in particular, deep down horses will always be at the forefront for me. They gave me a brilliant childhood, brought me to the Cotswolds, encouraged Aub to love them and became favourites with our children.

Animals have always been at the heart of everything we've done, and always will be. Our house is full of pictures of prizewinning sheep, mares and foals, dogs and cats interspersed with those of children and grandchildren, all part of our wonderful family.

Dash with her two foals

EPILOGUE

One Last Horse Story

Horses are always full of surprises. One of the saddest moments of my life, but also one of the most incredible, came from an incident that illustrated the love and understanding between my horses.

Millie, our original mare, now in her late teens, had given birth to Pablo, a beautiful skewbald colt. It was midnight, midsummer. She found it easier to get up and down on grass rather than a straw bed, due to her old injury, so we'd left her to foal outside, checking her at hourly intervals during the evening. A little while after she'd foaled the beautiful coloured colt, Aub and I walked them the few yards to the stable for the rest of the night. Happy and contented, we left them to bond.

In the morning I stroked the foal all over, as we always do so they are never worried about being handled. We were around the farm most of the morning, checking her often; new foals are real time wasters. After lunch, with Millie happily tucking into fresh hay and the foal suckling well, I gave mum a big kiss, told her I was collecting a friend's son from school and would be back before she ran out of hay.

On my return she wasn't looking over the stable door. I prepared to photograph mother and child lying down together. Imagine my shock when I looked over the door to see her lying dead with her foal still trying to suck from her.

Absolute panic. A frantic phone call to Aub and floods of hysterical tears. Why? How? Later, after talking with the vets, the obvious answer was internal bleeding, that we would have known nothing about, or a heart attack. She'd seemed perfectly alright when I left her. My lovely Millie. Mother of four of our beautiful foals and a delight to have on the place. Again, the loss of a horse was devastating.

More urgent was a replacement mother for a sixteen-hour old foal.

Joanna Varden at the foaling bank was so helpful, telling me to milk off what I could from the mare's udder as, if we had to transport the foal, he might need feeding on the way. Joanna didn't know of any local mares that had lost foals, so I rang a friend whose foal had had to be put down. She didn't think her mare had the temperament to take another foal, and knowing how difficult adoption can be with sheep, we decided not to go there. She did, however, suggest we tried our own mare Dash, who had foaled three weeks earlier, and offered to come over to help. Meanwhile Joanna had come back with the possibility of a mare in South Wales, and very kindly explained how to transport the foal, safely tied in a sack, to stop it damaging itself. The thought of such a trip horrified me.

With the help of our friend, I brought Dash and her bay filly foal into the adjacent stable. Dash and Millie were the greatest of friends. They'd lived and reared foals together for the past four years.

Our internal stables were really old calf boxes, with walls low enough for a horse to look over into the other box. As I led Dash in, she did just this, seeing Millie dead next door. My friend held Dash while Aub held her own foal slightly out of the way, and I persuaded Millie's colt out of his stable and into the next one. As he approached, Dash nickered to him. We didn't touch him or her. There was no need. Gently she pushed him with her soft white nose towards her udder and suckled him. We all watched in utter amazement. Adoptions don't normally happen like this. Gradually Dash moved over and Aub released her indignant filly, who immediately sucked the other side. Dash looked at me as if to say, 'ok, you can leave it now'.

Afterwards, we said she'd wanted a skewbald colt rather than a bay filly!

Obviously, I kept an eye on her behaviour for the next couple of hours, but we knew Dash. Not only was she 'probably the best brood mare in the country', but also the kindest.

Millie's colt, Pablo, never looked back.

About the Author

Sue **Andrews** is a journalist and sheep farmer. She has written for county magazines and the national equestrian and farming press.

She and her husband Aubrey have two children and they farm in Gloucestershire. They are internationally renowned breeders of both Texel and Blue Texel sheep. Sue tells the story of how their dream grew from small beginnings in *If Clouds Were Sheep (2019)*.

Jumping Over Clouds is her second book.

Three generations of sheepdogs

Acknowledgements

My thanks to everyone who has contributed to this story. My wonderful husband, children and their partners and all the grandchildren. A special 'thank you' to Leo for suggesting the title of this second book, just after I'd written the first. It works well.

My thanks to all those in the village of Miserden who have been so helpful with historic detail and reminded me of past years. While not all you've told me is shown in the book, I needed that background knowledge. Thank you Mary Griese MA for correcting my grammar and giving endless support.

My thanks to Dan for taking such lovely pictures of Dash, and Catherine for allowing me to use the picture of Aub at Three Counties Show.

And finally, although most importantly, thank you Lorna Gray for the magic of your brilliant editing ability, which has pulled this book together.

Also by Sue Andrews:

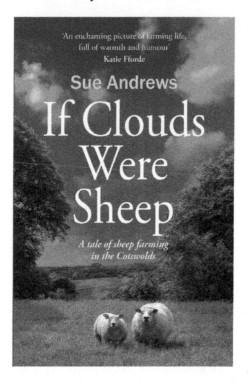

It seems an impossible dream at first for Sue and Aubrey.
She is a horse-mad girl strongly attracted to the idea of farming,
Aubrey is the son of a farm manager without land or money.
But with limited knowledge, much enthusiasm and the
challenge of raising their young family, anything can happen.

If Clouds Were Sheep

**This is where the story began:
a true story of the shepherding life –
amusing, poignant and beautifully detailed**